State of New York
Supreme Court, Appellate Division
Third Judicial Department

AF880686

Decided and Entered: August 21, 2014 519493

In the Matter of SAM SLOAN, as
Candidate for Governor of
the State of New York,
et al.,
Appellants,
v

MEMORANDUM AND ORDER

DOUGLAS A. KELLNER et al., as
Commissioners Constituting
the New York State Board of
Elections, et al.,
Respondents,
et al.,
Respondent.

Calendar Date: August 21, 2014

Before: McCarthy, J.P., Garry, Egan Jr., Lynch and Clark, JJ.

Neil Grimaldi, New York City, for appellants.

Kathleen O'Keefe, New York State Board of Elections, Albany, for Douglas A. Kellner and others, respondents.

Per Curiam.

Appeal from an order and judgment of the Supreme Court (Ceresia, J.), entered August 15, 2014 in Albany County, which dismissed petitioners' application, in a proceeding pursuant to Election Law § 16-102, to declare valid the designating petition naming petitioners Sam Sloan, Nenad Bach and Geeta Rankoth as Democratic Party candidates for certain statewide public offices in the September 9, 2014 primary election.

Petitioners, Sam Sloan, Nenad Bach and Geeta Rankoth, filed a designating petition nominating them as Democratic Party candidates for the respective public offices of Governor, Lieutenant Governor and Comptroller of the State of New York. The designating petition further nominates a nonparty, Neil V. Grimaldi, as Democratic Party candidate for the public office of Attorney General of the State of New York.[1] Objections were filed with regard to the candidacy of Rankoth and asserted, among other things, that the petition contained fewer than one third of the 15,000 signatures required for any of the four candidacies (see Election Law § 6-136 [1]). The New York State Board of Elections agreed and invalidated the designating petition in its entirety. Petitioners thereafter commenced this proceeding seeking a declaration that the State Board's composition is unconstitutional and an order directing that they be included on the primary ballot. Supreme Court dismissed the petition, and petitioners appeal.

We affirm. As Supreme Court properly found, the present proceeding is jurisdictionally defective due to the "failure to name and serve all those who filed objections to the designating petition" (Matter of Gadsen v Board of Elections of City of N.Y., 57 NY2d 751, 752 [1982]; see Matter of Biscone v Scaringe, 59 AD2d 794, 794 [1977], affd 42 NY2d 1075 [1977]).

Assuming without deciding that the above jurisdictional defect only applies to Rankoth – against whose candidacy objections were filed – petitioners also argue that the composition of the State Board does not give equal weight to each voter as required by the Equal Protection Clause of the 14th Amendment to the US Constitution (see Reynolds v Sims, 377 US 533, 560-561 [1964]). They are incorrect, as the underlying principle of one vote per person does not apply to an appointive board, especially where it is charged with administrative duties (see Rosenthal v Board of Educ. of Cent. School Dist. No. 3 of Town of Hempstead, 497 F2d 726, 729 [2d Cir 1974]; see also Hadley v Junior College Dist. of Metropolitan Kansas City, 397 US

---

[1] Grimaldi's application to be added as a petitioner was denied by Supreme Court as untimely.

50, 54 [1970]; Sailors v Board of Educ. of County of Kent, 387 US 105, 111 [1967]; compare Board of Estimate of City of N.Y. v Morris, 489 US 688, 694-696 [1989]). The State Board was thus properly constituted, and was free to hold that the designating petition, which lacked the necessary number of signatures to support any of petitioners' candidacies, was facially defective and invalid in its entirety (see Election Law § 6-154 [1]; Matter of Hunting v Power, 54 Misc 2d 120, 122 [1967], affd 28 AD2d 826 [1967], affd 20 NY2d 680 [1967]).

Petitioners' remaining arguments have been considered and found to lack merit.

McCarthy, J.P., Garry, Egan Jr., Lynch and Clark, JJ., concur.

ORDERED that the order and judgment is affirmed, without costs.

ENTER:

Robert D. Mayberger
Clerk of the Court

SUPREME COURT OF THE STATE OF NEW YORK

APPELLATE DIVISION - THIRD DEPARTMENT

In the Matter of the Application of Sam Sloan, as Candidate for Governor of the State of New York, Nenad Bach as Candidate for Lieutenant Governor of the State of New York, Geeta Rankoth as Candidate for Comptroller of the State of New York and Neil v. Grimaldi as Candidate for Attorney General of the State of New York

Petitioners-Candidates-Aggrieved

BRIEF FOR PETITIONERS

-against-

DOUGLAS A. KELLNER, ANDREW SPANO, JAMES A. WALSH and GREGORY P. PETERSON Commissioners and Constituting the NEW YORK STATE BOARD OF ELECTIONS

Index No. 4003-14

Respondents

ERIC T. SCHNEIDERMAN as Attorney General of the State of New York

---

For an Order Pursuant to Sections 16-100, 16-102 and 16-116 of the Election Law Declaring Valid the Designating Petitions purporting to Designate SAM SLOAN, NENAD BACH, GEETA RANKOTH and NEIL V. GRIMALDI as candidates for the Democratic Party nomination for Governor, Lieutenant Governor. Comptroller of New York State and attorney General of New York State respectfully at the Primary Election to be held at September 9, 2014 and restoring them to the Official Ballots of Such Primary Election

---

PRELIMINARY STATEMENT

Petitioners appeal from an August 12, 2014 judgment of the Supreme Court Albany County by Acting Supreme Court Judge Andrew G. Ceresia. By that judgment Petitioner-Appellants were removed from the ballot confirming the ruling by the New York Board of Elections which found petitioners had insufficient signatures.

INTRODUCTION

Petitioners Designating Petitions were filed timely on July 8, 2014. The Board of Elections marked them valid. The case presented at the

Supreme Court failed to enter any specifications of objections required by Election Law 16-102 against Sam Sloan, Nenad Bach or Neil V. Grimaldi. There were no specifications of objections entered by Respondent as to insufficient signatures of these candidates.

There were only Specifications of Objections filed against Geeta Rankoth for her insufficient age to be Comptroller which the petitioners accept. However, the petitioners want to replace her through the Committee on Vacancies on the Designating Petitions.

The Petitioners hold that since there were no Objections or Specifications filed against the other candidates they should be permitted to be on the ballot.

There were no Objections or Specifications filed at the Board against Sam Sloan so petitioners argue that there was no basis to exclude him from the ballot. To do so without any notice or a hearing in regard to his petitions violates his Due Process rights under the Fourteenth Amendment.

The court heard of No Specifications or Objections against any other candidate as required by New York Election Law so there is no basis for invalidating their candidacy.

The petitioners hold that the petition signers had United States Constitutional Rights to have candidates of their choices. Their is no basis in this court to invalidate their constitutional rights as federal case law. See <u>Reynolds vs. Sims</u> 377 US 533, <u>Baker vs. Carr</u>, 369 US 186 .

The petitioners herein hold that there were no witnesses called at the Board hearing to justify the invalidating of these designating petitions. The only thing that happened was that an attorney Kimberly Galven stated that we are going to throw off these candidates. Despite the fact that Kimberly Galvin is a paid for the Board of Elections whose office is at 40 North Pearl Street in Albany and only a few blocks from the Supreme Court Albany County at 16 Eagle Street, Miss Galvin was not called as an witness to contradict the testimony of Sam Sloan, a reputable person and mathematician who testified as to his credentials to establish his uncontradicted testimony.

The Board pursuant to Mr. Sam Sloan's uncontradicted testimony violated the due process clause of the Fourteenth Amendment and made a decision without any witnesses. Or falsified based on or even following the basic constitutional requirement of a board as to substantiate their decision. The Board never even examined the designating petitions so even if they try to hold they were insufficient especially without a sworn statement when Miss Galvin was never a sworn witness.

Also the court entered into evidence improperly copies not the original designating petitions. The copies were not even the same size or the same thickness. An examination of the Designating Petitions produced to the court would clearly indicate if they are comparable to that which were entered improperly over objection into evidence.

There was no valid basis at the Board hearing to violate the United States Constitutional rights of the designating petition signers or the candidates on the designating petitions.

Petitioners have sought to invalidate the New York Board of Elections because all the power at the board is given to Republican and Democratic members evenly even though Democrats are more populace than Republicans. Also, the fact that millions of voters who are independent or are members of parties who have no ballot access have no representation on the New York Board of Elections. Also, in New York City, Staten Island has the same amount of representatives, one, as do the more populated boroughs. This was the exact reason specified in Board of Estimate of City of New York v. Morris 489 U.S. 688 (1988) decided: March 22, 1989, that was found to be unconstitutional. This is what the petitioners seek this court to determine.

POINT ONE

The New York State Board of Elections as well as the various city and local county boards should be invalidated pursuant to the law and the ends of justice.

1) In Board of Estimate of City of New York v. Morris 489 U.S. 688 (1988) decided: March 22, 1989, the United States Supreme Court held as I am seeking which is the law of the United States. The United States Supreme Court held the Board of Estimates was illegally constituted because it violated the Equal Protection Clause of the 14th Amendment to the constitution. So, the New York Board of Estimates was found to be null and void as a government agency, citing Reynolds vs. Sims, 377 US 533 and Abate vs Muss, 403 US 182. The Board of Elections completely denies voter equality by ignoring the voting rights of all voters, not Republican or Democrat. Also, Republican Voters have more voting power than Democrats because Democrats far exceed Republican voters. The NY Board of Elections and the New York City Board of Elections violate the Equal Protection Clause based on the disparity between Republicans and Democrats and the fact that so many millions of voters have no representative on the Board of Elections. This inequitable system at the board places the most prejudicial people as executives or board members by how they are chosen by representatives of the Democratic Party

Chairperson and Republican Party Chairperson. Therefore, they cannot constitute a just body or forum to make legal and binding decisions.

This year at a recent July 2014 hearing of the New York City Board of Elections, Eliot Quinones was placed on the ballot by the clerk's report. Then without notice a new Board of Elections clerk's report put him off the ballot. These decisions excluded voters who properly signed the petition. New York Board of Elections clerk's report fundamentally put him off the ballot based on improper decisions excluding voters who properly signed the petition. The New York City Board of Elections also allows one representative and one representative for Brooklyn despite the fact that Brooklyn has three times as many voters as Richmond. This is exactly the reason why the Board of Estimates was found illegal by the United States Supreme Court. The Board of Elections in the City of New York is part of the New York State Board of Elections.

2) Reynolds vs Sims, 377 US 533 established that the Fourteenth Amendment of the United States Constitution established the principle of the equal protection clause and equal protection of the law. Required the Alabama legislature voting to be based on population. The Board of Elections ignores this landmark case and principle. This case stands for the fundamental principle of legislative government in the United States of equal representation for equal numbers of people. The right to vote is a personal right. The idea that one

group can be granted greater voting strength as the board does excluding all Democratic and Republican voters than another is inconsistent with standards for popular representative government. Under the equal protection clause a claim of debasement of the right to vote through mal apportionment represents a practicable controversy. And the equal protection clause provides manageable standards for the lower courts to determine the constitutionality of a state legislative appointment scheme, citing Baker vs. Carr, 361 US 186. In addition it undercuts states voters rights and the duly established United States Constitutional rights.

3) Oliver vs. Board of Education, 306 F. Supp. 1286, No. 69 Civ 2130, United States District Court for the Southern District of New York held that a statute creating the New York City School Board was unconstitutional where the statute provided that citizens of each borough elected one member of the school board. Statute diluted votes of the most populous boroughs. The way the New York State Board of Elections and New York City Board of Elections is organized violates the rights of all voters not Republican or Democratic and gives each Republican voter more power than each Democrat which is unequal and illegal. Also, voting procedures including proxy voting must follow one man one vote Atkins v. Monahan, 91 Misc. 2d 499, 399 NYS 2d 166.

4) Sergey v. King's County Republican Party, 459 F.2d 308 invalidated a county political party's rule on the voting procedure of the one

party where each county committee member has an equal vote weighed according to the number of Republican voters in the district he represents. This violates the one-man one-vote principle established by the Supreme Court as a voters constitutional right. The amount of Democratic Party voters far exceeds the amount of Republican Party voters and gives one Republican and Democratic members equal power and not representing all other voters and Republican or Democratic violated the one-man one-vote constitutional law principle. The equal protection clause applies one man one vote even to count committeemen. Not giving a group the right to representation violates their constitutional rights and discriminates against them. See Moder v. Ogilive 394 US 814, 89 S.Ct. 1493

5) Fisher vs. Board of Supervisors, 59 Misc. 953; 301 NYS 2d 310 citing Seaman v. Fedourich, 16 NY 2d 94, 101 required the "one man one vote" principle required each votes be given equal weight. The Board of Elections excludes the rights of millions of voters and unfairly gives Republican voters more importance than an equal number of Democratic voters. See Burton vs. Schmidt, 128 Misc. 270.

6) The basic exclusion of the Board of Elections of the rights of millions of voters not Republican and Democrat is unequitably a violation of the equal protection clause of the Fourteenth Amendment see Reynolds vs. Sims, supra, Board of Estimates vs. Morris, supra.

7) The New York City Board of Elections has a long history of violating the United States voter's rights and insurgent Democratic and Republican voters rights including none of the other parties by the illegal manner that members of the Board of Elections in New York City as elsewhere are chosen by the New York City Republican and Democratic Party political readers. This violates the Fourteenth Amendment due process requirements because the forum is not a just body and it is constituted in a way by giving undue and improper power to representatives of the Democratic and Republican Chairmen and their representatives who claim to me made a quasi-judicial body making legally binding decisions which they have harmful by their extensive officer and bureau members are selected illegally by the Political Democratic Party Chairmen and Republican Chairmen. It would be proper and legal only to have a civil service Board of Elections. The members of the Board of Elections or an independent non-partisan non-prejudicial system of choosing Board of Election members statewide and in New York City and in each of our great New York County.

8) <u>The Respondents have refused to provide a legal basis in opposition to this motion because there is none.</u>

Whereas Petitioner is requesting an opportunity to subpoena witnesses and present evidence about the long history of political corruption caused by the illegal and improper manner the New York State Board of

Elections and New York City Board of Elections are illegally formed, violative of the equal protection clause one man one vote and basic justice.

POINT TWO

The New York State Board of Elections at their August 1, 2014 meeting and the subsequent Albany Court proceeding on August 11, 2012 were not sufficient to violate the constitutional rights of the Designating Petition signers or the Candidates of their choices or the rights of these candidates to be on the ballot.

The designating petition signers have established and protected United States Constitutional Rights to have the candidates they favor by signing their petition. See Reynolds vs. Sims 377 US 533, Baker vs. Carr, 369 US 186 .

The proceeding at the Board of Elections violates the due process clause of the Fourteenth Amendment rights of these candidates and their designated signers.

1) There was no evidence legally or properly produced to invalidate these petitions.

2) There was no testimony by anyone even Miss Kimberly Galvin

saying we have to throw these designating petitions off the ballot.

3) The board members did not examine the petitions but improperly and illegally based their statement on a paid lawyer representing the Republican party, not a non-partial witness and there was no testimony to justify their actions to violate the US Constitutional Rights of the designating petition voters and their candidates.

4) The court had no basis to allow in minimized copied designating petitions. The respondent Board has said originals and was obligated to produce them. The substitution of these minimized copies from the originals was fraudulent.

CONCLUSION

1) The Board of Elections of the State of New York must be found unconstitutional and eliminated as was the Board of Estimates of the City of New York by the United States Supreme Court and for the same factual and legal reasons.

2) The board failed to properly give consideration failing to require Objections and Specifications and failed to provide Fourteenth Amendment due process of law. They violated the United States Constitutional Rights to due process of law.

Respectfully Submitted,

DATED: August 14, 2014

Bronx, New York

Neil Grimaldi, Esq.

Attorney for Petitioners-Candidates

2860 Buhre Avenue, 1E

Bronx NY 10461

646-229-7974

Affidavit of Service

Neil Grimaldi, a New York attorney, states:

the law brief has been faxed to the New Yor k Board of Elections at 40 North Pearl Street, Albany New York on August 8, 2014

DATED: August 14, 2014

Bronx, New York

____

Neil Grimaldi, Esq.

Attorney for Petitioners-Candidates

2860 Buhre Avenue, 1E

Bronx NY 10461

646-229-7974

SUPREME COURT OF THE STATE OF NEW YORK
COUNTY OF ALBANY

In the Matter of the Application of Sam Sloan, as Candidate for Governor of the State of New York, Nenad Bach as Candidate for Lieutenant Governor of the State of New York and Geeta Rankoth as Candidate for Comptroller of the State of New York

Petitioners-Candidates-Aggrieved

REPLY BRIEF

-against-

Index No. 4003-14

DOUGLAS A. KELLNER, ANDREW SPANO, JAMES A. WALSH and GREGORY P. PETERSON Commissioners and Constituting the NEW YORK STATE BOARD OF ELECTIONS

Respondents

ERIC T. SCHNEIDERMAN as Attorney General of the State of New York

For an Order Pursuant to Sections 16-100, 16-102 and 16-116 of the Election Law Declaring Valid the Designating Petitions purporting to Designate SAM SLOAN, NENAD BACH and GEETA RANKOTH as candidates for the Democratic Party nomination for Governor, Lieutenant Governor and Comptroller of New York State, respectfully at the Primary Election to be held at September 9, 2014 and restoring them to the Official Ballots of Such Primary Election

TO THE SUPREME COURT OF THE STATE OF NEW YORK:

COUNTY OF ALBANY

POINT ONE

The Judge's decision failed to differentiate between between an educational administrative body and the New York Board of Elections, which is an executive body with quasi-judicial functions

and decides issues involving the United States Constitutional Rights of Voters to their choice of candidates and the candidate's United States rights.

The Board of Estimates vs. Morris 489 US 688 (1988) governs this case rather than the much earlier decision of <u>Sailors et al vs. Board of Education of Kent et al</u>, 387 US 105 (1967) because the New York State Board of Elections is much more similar to the Board of Estimates of the City of New York and the fact is that the Board of Estimates case is later.

The case of <u>Sailors, supra</u> concerned only the election of county school board members whose electors are elected by the people. Where a school board member has a non-legislative office for which no election is involved or required. The Sailors case required "a subordinate governmental instrumentality created by the state to assist in carrying out of state governmental functions.

The court in Sailors based their decision on the fact that the work done by the Kent County was basically minor.

The Board of Elections of New York has a quasi-judicial functions invalidating candidates from the ballot and this involve decisions regarding United States Constitutional rights of voters and candidate,

Therefore the standard is "one man one vote " is the established law of the nation, <u>Gray v. Saunders</u> 372 U.S. 368, <u>Reynolds v Sims</u> 377 U,S,533; <u>Baker v. Carr</u> 369 U.S.186; <u>Guttney v Cummins</u> 412 U.S. 735; <u>Seaman v Fedourich</u> 16 N.Y. 2d 44; <u>Moder v Ogilve</u> 394 U.S. 814, <u>Oliver v Bd of Education</u> 306 F Supp 1286.

Restraints imposed by the constitution on the states can never be circumvented by local bodies to

whom the state delegates authority like The Board of Elections for the State of New York and the Board of Elections for The City of New York. Standard Computing Scale Company v Farrell 249 U.S. 577; Cooper v Aaron 358 U.S. 1,17.

The other case the judge cited is Cohanim vs. New York City Board of Education, 204 F. Supp. 2d 452, 453 (2002) involved only how New York City Board of Education members are selected. Their Education Board is in no way comparable to the New York State Board of Elections which has quasi-judicial and executive functions regarding the United States Constitutional Rights of voters in having candidates of their choice and the United States Constitutional Rights of candidates.

In Hedley vs. Junior College District, 397 US 50, the United States Supreme Court dispensed with the standard set forth in Sailors, supra and held that the election to a position that performed a governmental function as the New York States Board of Elections does must accord with "one man one vote"

The Fourteenth Amendment section 1 states "nor deny any person within its jurisdiction the equal protection of the law" All voters including members of all other parties other than Republican or Democratic have no voice or representation on the Board of Elections and deprives them of equal protection of the laws. The Board of Estimate v Morris, supra.

The equal protection clause forbids the elevation of a small class of super-voters granted an extraordinary powerful franchise as does the Board of Elections for Republican and Democratic only voters. Brown v Tonson 462 U.S. 835 (1083)

The Board of Elections not representing smaller parties violates minority rights of smaller parties as set forth in Section 2 of The Federal Voting Rights Act 42 U.S. 1973 et seq,

The New York State Board of Elections and their local boards must be held unconstitutional because they fail to represent millions of voters and they violate "one man one vote" Dunn v Blumstein 408 U,S, 330 (1972); Abate v Mundt 403 U.S. 182.

The fact The Board makes quasi-judicial decisions and is made up of members who have an interest in the outcome makes them an unfair judicial body thus violating procedural due process of the Fourteenth Amendment. The Board members chosen by the chairmen of the Republican and Democratic parties is especially prejudicial when they vote on issues of ballot access who are the individuals who appointed them as this slate of candidates including Sam Sloan for Governor has done.

The Board of Elections could not heretofore produce one valid and sustainable legal precedent for the continuation of The Board of Elections in the face of all the existing cases cited herein that prove and illustrates clearly that The Board violates The Equal Protection Clause and "one man one vote"legal precedents that protect individuals like the petition signers and all the candidates that are on this slate as Petitioners .Reynolds v Sims; Connor v. Finch, 431 U.S. 407, 420 (1977); Cohen v Mahoney,410 F. Supp 1286; Grisbaum v. McKeithen, 339 F. Supp. 267 (1971), Latino Political Action Commitee, Inc. vs. City of Boston, 784 F.2d 409 (1986); Iannucci v. Bd. of Supervisors of Washington County, 20 N.Y. 2D 244,249: Franklin v Mandeville ,26 N.Y. 2D 65, 69-70; Franklin v Krause 32 N.Y. 2D 234; Westberry v Sanders 403 U.S. 1; Curcio v Boyle 147 A.D. 194; Jackson v Nassau County Bd. of Supervisors, 818 F. Supp. 98; Very v Midland County 390 U.S. 547, Whitcomb v Chavis 403 U.S. 124,145-146 (1976) Karcher v Daggett, 46 U.S. 725,741

(1971).

POINT TWO

The Supreme Court had insufficient evidence as a matter of law to invalidate these candidates from being on the ballot and violating the United States constitutional rights of their petition signers and The Board of Elections violated procedural due process in invalidating the petitions without notice to the Petioner - Candidates and not having a viable hearing at The Board as required by The Fourteenth Amendment and the due process clause. Goldberg v Kelly;397 U. S. 284; Bell v Bunson 402 U.S. 535, Sherber v Verner, 374 U.S, 374 U.S. 309.

Dated: August 21, 2014
Bronx NY

Respectfully submitted,

Neil V. Grimaldi
2860 Buhre Ave 1E
Bronx NY 10461

646-229-7974

519493

STATE OF NEW YORK	APPELLATE DIVISION
SUPREME COURT	THIRD DEPARTMENT

In the Matter of the Application of SAM SLOAN, as Candidate for Governor of the State of New York, NENAD BACH, as Candidate for Lieutenant Governor of the State of New York and GEETA RANKOTH, as Candidate for Comptroller of the State of New York,

Petitioners-Appellants,

v

DOUGLAS A. KELLNER, ANDREW SPANO, JAMES A. WALSH, and GREGORY O. PETERSON, as Commissioners and Constituting the NEW YORK STATE BOARD OF ELECTIONS, ERIC T. SCHNEIDERMAN, as Attorney General of the State of New York,

Respondents-Respondents.

RECORD ON APPEAL

Neil Grimaldi, Esq.
Attorney for Appellants
2860 Buhre Avenue
Bronx, NY 10461
(646) 229-7974

Kathleen O'Keefe, Esq.
Attorney for Respondents
New York State Board of Elections
40 North Pearl Street
Albany, NY 12207-2108

TABLE OF CONTENTS

Petitioners-Candidates-Aggrieved

And

DOUGLAS A. KELLNER, ANDREW SPANO, JAMES A. WALSH and GREGORY P. PETERSON Commissioners and Constituting the NEW YORK STATE BOARD OF ELECTIONS

Respondents

ERIC T. SCHNEIDERMAN as Attorney General of the State of New York Respondents

There has been no change in the parties except that NEIL V. GRIMALDI has been added as a petitioner-candidate-aggrieved

3. This proceeding was commenced in Supreme Court, Albany County.

4. This proceeding was commenced on August 4, 2014 by service of an Order to Show Cause

5. This is an election laws case. It is for an For an Order Pursuant to Sections 16-100, 16-102 and 16-116 of the Election Law Declaring Valid the Designating Petitions purporting to

Designate SAM SLOAN, NENAD BACH, GEETA RANKOTH and NEIL V. GRIMALDI as candidates for the Democratic Party nomination for Governor, Lieutenant Governor, Comptroller and Attorney General of New York State, respectfully at the Primary Election to be held at September 9, 2014 and restoring them to the Official Ballots of Such Primary Election

6. This is an appeal from an order of Hon. Andrew G. Ceresia entered in favor of respondents which denied the petition to Validate.

7. This appeal is on the original record

DATED: August 13, 2014
Bronx, New York

Neil Grimaldi, Esq.
Attorney for Petitioners-Candidates
2860 Buhre Avenue, 1E
Bronx NY 10461

646-229-7974

SUPREME COURT OF THE STATE OF NEW YORK Albs

ALBANY COUNTy

In the matter of application of Sam Sloan ,et al

,Petitioners

against

NOTICE OF APPEAL

4003-14

Board of Elections of The Stat of New York

And Eric Schneiderman as New York Attorney General

Respondents

PLEASE TAKE NOTICE that petitioners hereby appeal to the Supreme Court, Appelate Division,Third J judicial Department from the judgment rendered in Supreme Court, Albany County Auguest 12,2014 by Judge Andrew A.Cisneras on August 12,2014 and from each and every part rtherof and every intermediate part therein.

Dated: August 13 2014

Bronx, New York

Neil Grimaldi

Neil Grimaldi

2860 Buhre Av. 1E

Bronx, N.Y. 10461

To: New York Board of Elections

49 North Pearl Streer, Albany, New York

ALBANY COUNTY CLERK
PAID
6

Albany County Clerk
Document Number 11675254
Rcvd 08/18/2014 1:58:41 PM

STATE OF NEW YORK
SUPREME COURT   COUNTY OF ALBANY

In the Matter of the Application of
SAM SLOAN, as Candidate for Governor of the State of New York, NENAD BACH, as Candidate for Lieutenant Governor of the State of New York, and GEETA RANKOTH, as Candidate for Comptroller of the State of New York,

Petitioners,

-against-

DECISION/ORDER/ JUDGMENT

DOUGLAS A. KELLNER, ANDREW SPANO, JAMES A. WALSH, and GREGORY P. PETERSON, Commissioners and Constituting the NEW YORK STATE BOARD OF ELECTIONS, and ERIC T. SCHNEIDERMAN, Attorney General of the State of New York,

Respondents.

All Purpose Term
Hon. Andrew G. Ceresia, Acting Supreme Court Justice
Index No. 4003-14

Appearances:[1]

Neil Grimaldi, Esq.
Attorney for Petitioners
2860 Buhre Avenue
Bronx, New York 10461

Kathleen O'Keefe, Esq.
For Respondent New York State
Board of Elections
40 North Pearl Street
Albany, New York 12207-2108

---

1 Although the Attorney General was a named respondent and was served with the petition, that office advised the Court that it would not be participating in this matter.

Ceresia, J.

Petitioners, arguing that respondent New York State Board of Elections (hereinafter "the Board") improperly invalidated their designating petitions as Democratic Party candidates for statewide offices, commenced the above-captioned proceeding pursuant to Election Law § 16-100 *et seq.* to validate their designating petitions. Petitioners also seek to have the Board declared null and void as violative of the federal constitution and federal law. Finally, petitioners seek attorney's fees. The Board opposed, asserting that petitioners' designating petitions were invalidated because they contained fewer than the minimum number of required signatures, and because petitioner Geeta Rankoth was found not to be of the minimum age required to hold the office of Comptroller.

The Court held a hearing on August 11, 2014, for the purpose of allowing the parties to be heard further and/or present evidence. Petitioners elicited sworn testimony from petitioner Sam Sloan, without objection from the Board. The Board offered into evidence copies of two sets of general and specific objections by Victor Perez and Scott Bailey (Exhibits 2 and 3, respectively), copies of petitioners' designating petitions (Exhibit 4), and a certification indicating that the aforementioned documents were true and exact copies of the originals (Exhibit 1). Petitioners asserted specific objections to the admission of these documents, arguing that the documents should not come into evidence because the Board is unconstitutionally organized and was without authority to act in the absence of objections. Petitioners, however, did not raise any foundational objections or any other objections impacting the admissibility of the documents. As such, the Court overruled petitioners' objections – which, again, bore no relevance to the actual admissibility of the documents in question – and received the exhibits into evidence.[2]

Turning first to the candidacy of Grimaldi – petitioners' counsel, who seeks to run for the office of New York State Attorney General – it is noted that Grimaldi was not named as a party in the petition commencing this proceeding. Rather, in the same affidavit/motion which set forth petitioners' best evidence objection, petitioners also for the first time seek to add Grimaldi as a named petitioner. Noting that the return date in this matter has passed and the hearing has already been concluded, this application is denied as untimely. In any event, even if Grimaldi were to be added as a named petitioner, he still would not be entitled to the relief that he seeks, for the same reasons set forth below with respect to petitioners Sam Sloan and Nenad Bach.

2

On August 12, 2014, the day after the hearing was concluded, petitioners faxed to the Court an unsworn affidavit/motion from Neil Grimaldi, Esq. No indication has been provided to the Court that said affidavit/motion was served on respondents. Pursuant to the affidavit/motion, petitioners argue for the first time that the best evidence rule prohibited admission into evidence of copies of the designating petitions (Exhibit 4). This objection is untimely. In that regard, the Court notes that, had that objection been raised in a timely manner during the hearing as it was required to be, the Board would have had the chance to be heard on the matter, the Court would have had the opportunity to make a ruling, and the Board ultimately would have had the chance to cure the defect, if any. Accordingly, the petitioners' untimely best evidence objection is now overruled.

Next, with respect to the candidacy of Geeta Rankoth, the instant petition is jurisdictionally defective because, although objections were filed to Rankoth's designating petitions, Rankoth failed to name and serve the objectors, who are necessary parties to a proceeding to validate designating petitions (see Matter of Gadsen v Bd. of Elec. of City of N.Y., 57 NY2d 751, 752 [1982]; Matter of Plochocki v Onondaga County Board of Elections, 21 AD3d 710, 710 [2005]; Matter of Fusco v Westchester County Bd. of Elec., 286 AD2d 456, 456-457 [2001], lv denied 96 NY2d 718 [2001]). Nevertheless, even considering the merits of the petition as it relates to Rankoth, the Board properly ruled that Rankoth's designating petitions were invalid because Rankoth did not meet the age requirement to hold the office of New York State Comptroller, and because her designating petitions contained fewer than the minimum number of signatures. Petitioners concede that Rankoth is too young for the position, and the record reveals that Rankoth's designating petitions contained only 4,087 signatures, far short of the necessary 15,000 (see Election Law § 6-136 [1]). Therefore, the instant petition is denied as it pertains to Rankoth.

With regard to petitioners' further argument that Rankoth should be replaced by a committee on vacancies rather than having her petitions invalidated, "a designated committee to fill vacancies may act only if the designating petition itself is deemed valid" (Matter of Elgin v Smith, 10 AD3d 483, 484 [2004]; see Matter of Owens v Sharpton, 45 NY2d 794, 795 [1978]; Matter of Marcatante v Lundy, 8 Misc 2d 313, 316-317 [1957], affd 4 AD2d 883 [1957]). Here, since Rankoth's designating petitions were invalid, the committee on vacancies is not empowered to name a replacement candidate.

Turning to the candidacies of Sloan and Bach, petitioners claim that the Board acted beyond the scope of its authority and in an arbitrary and capricious manner by invalidating their designating petitions without any objections having been filed. However, under Election Law § 6-154 (1), the Board has the authority to perform a ministerial, facial review of designating petitions to determine whether they are in the proper form and appear to bear the requisite number of signatures (see Matter of Rosen v McNab, 25 NY2d 798, 799 [1969]; Matter of Mansfield v Epstein, 5 NY2d 70, 73 [1958]). The Board may make such a determination even in the absence of objections (see Casler v Bd. of Elec. of Herkimer County, 131 Misc 744, 746 [1928]; see also Jerry H. Goldfeder, Goldfeder's Modern Election Law § 4 [C], at 37; 50 NY Jur 2d Elections § 371). Here, the Board acted properly in conducting a facial review of the designating petitions and then invalidating said petitions on the basis that they did not contain the requisite number of signatures. In that regard, it is noted that even the most cursory facial review of the designating petitions clearly reveals that they could not possibly contain the necessary 15,000 signatures. That is, the last numbered page of the submitted designating petitions was 1,402, and each page allotted for no more than 10 signatures. Thus, even 1,402 pages with 10 signatures on each page would fall approximately 1,000 signatures short of what was needed. Further, there are numerous and significant gaps in pagination such that it is clear that there were significantly fewer than 1,402 pages of designating petitions filed. In addition to that, numerous pages contain fewer than the full allotment of 10 signatures. Therefore, it is clear that the Board acted well within the scope of its authority, was not arbitrary or capricious, and properly invalidated the designating petitions for lack of signatures, even in the absence of objections. Accordingly, the instant petition is denied with respect to Sloan and Bach.

As a final matter, petitioners argue that the composition of the Board violates the federal constitution and federal law because it is made up only of Democrats and Republicans, with no representation by independent voters or minor party members, and thus violates the "one man, one vote" principle. However, "[s]ince the choice of members of the [Board] did not involve an election and since none was required for these nonlegislative offices, the principle of 'one man, one vote' has no relevancy" (Sailors v Bd. of Ed. of Kent County, 387 US 105, 111 [1967]; see Cohanim v New York City Bd. of Ed., 204 F Supp 2d 452, 453 [2002] [holding that the "one person, one vote" standard does not apply to appointed bodies]). As such, petitioners' claim in this regard is without merit.

Accordingly, it is hereby

ORDERED AND ADJUDGED that the petition is denied.

This shall constitute the decision and order of the Court. The original decision and order is returned to the attorney for BOE. All other papers are being delivered to the Supreme Court Clerk for delivery to the County Clerk or directly to the County Clerk for filing. The signing of this decision and order and delivery of this decision and order does not constitute entry or filing under CPLR Rule 2220. Counsel is not relieved from the applicable provisions of that rule respecting filing, entry and notice of entry.

DATED: August 12, 2014
Troy, New York

Andrew G. Ceresia
Acting Supreme Court Justice

Papers Considered:

1. Verified Petition dated August 4, 2014;
2. Letter of Helena Lynch, Esq., dated August 6, 2014;
3. Letter of Kathleen O'Keefe, Esq., dated August 7, 2014, and Exhibits;
4. Letter of Frank G. Hoare, Esq., dated August 7, 2014, and Exhibits.
5. Statement of Law of Neil Grimaldi, Esq., dated August 8, 2014;
6. Affidavit/Motion of Neil Grimaldi, Esq., dated August 11, 2014, received August 12, 2014.

At a Special Term of The Supreme Court of the State of New York, held in and for the County of Albany, at the Supreme Courthouse thereof, on the 4th day of August, 2014

PRESENT: Gerald W. Connolly
HON:

In the Matter of the Application of Sam Sloan, as Candidate for Governor of the State of New York, Nenad Bach as Candidate for Lieutenant Governor of the State of New York and Geeta Rankoth as Candidate for Comptroller of the State of New York

Petitioners-Candidates-Aggrieved

-against-

DOUGLAS A. KELLNER, ANDREW SPANO, JAMES A. WALSH and GREGORY P. PETERSON Commissioners and Constituting the NEW YORK STATE BOARD OF ELECTIONS
Respondents

ERIC T. SCHNEIDERMAN as Attorney General of the State of New York

ORDER TO SHOW CAUSE TO VALIDATE DESIGNATING PETITIONS
Index No. 4003-14

For an Order Pursuant to Sections 16-100, 16-102 and 16-116 of the Election Law Declaring Valid the Designating Petitions purporting to Designate SAM SLOAN, NENAD BACH and GEETA RANKOTH as candidates for the Democratic Party nomination for Governor, Lieutenant Governor and Comptroller of New York State, respectfully at the Primary Election to be held at September 9, 2014 and restoring them to the Official Ballots of Such Primary Election

---

Upon the annexed verified petition of Neil Grimaldi and Sam

Sloan duly verified the 4th day of August, 2014 and upon the original Democratic Party designating petitions purporting to designate Sam Sloan as Candidate for the Democratic Party nomination for Governor, Nenad Bach as Candidate for the Democratic Party nomination for Lieutenant Governor and Geeta Rankoth as Candidate for the Democratic Party nomination for Comptroller of New York State respectfully and upon all of the papers and proceedings had herein:

LET the Respondents named herein above show cause before this court at a Special Term for Election Proceedings at be held at the A;bany County and Supreme Court Courthouse, 16 Eagle Street, Albany New York on the 7th day of August, 2014 at 2:00 ~~AM~~ P.M. of that day or as soon thereafter as counsel can be heard why an order should not be made and entered herein: *Personal Appearance Required GWC 8/4/14

1. Declaring sufficient and valid the designating petitions filed with the New York State Board of Elections purporting to designate and/or nominate Sam Sloan as Candidate for the Democratic Party nomination for Governor, Nenad Bach as Candidate for the Democratic Party nomination for Lieutenant Governor and Geeta Rankoth as Candidate for the Democratic Party nomination for Comptroller of New York State to be held on September 9, 2014 and

2. Ordering and decreeing and directing the New York State Board of Elections to restore the names of Sam Sloan,

9

Nenad Bach and Geeta Rankoth to the ballot as Candidates for the Democratic Party nomination for Governor, Lieutenant Governor and Comptroller of New York State to be printed and placed on the official ballots to be used either at the September 9, 2014 Democratic Primary Election and the November 4, 2014 General Election and why the Petitioners should not have such other and further relief as to this court may seem just and proper.

SUFFICIENT CAUSE APPEARING THEREFOR, it is ordered that service of a copy of this order together with a copy of the papers upon which it is based by delivery to the Board of Elections of the state of New York at 40 N. Pearl Street, Suite 5, Albany New York 12207 or by mailing it to their offices at the above address on or before the 5th day of August 2014 and service of this order on the office of Eric T. Schneiderman as Attorney General of the State of New York before the 5th day of August 2014 be deemed good and sufficient service.

ENTER:

HON. Gerald W. Connolly

JUSTICE OF THE SUPREME COURT

OF THE STATE OF NEW YORK

10

SUPREME COURT OF THE STATE OF NEW YORK
COUNTY OF ALBANY

In the Matter of the Application of Sam Sloan, as Candidate for Governor of the State of New York, Nenad Bach as Candidate for Lieutenant Governor of the State of New York and Geeta Rankoth as Candidate for Comptroller of the State of New York

Petitioners-Candidates-Aggrieved

-against-

DOUGLAS A. KELLNER, ANDREW SPANO, JAMES A. WALSH and GREGORY P. PETERSON Commissioners and Constituting the NEW YORK STATE BOARD OF ELECTIONS
Respondents

ERIC T. SCHNEIDERMAN as Attorney General of the State of New York

---

PETITION TO VALIDATE DESIGNATING PETITIONS
Index No.
4003-14

For an Order Pursuant to Sections 16-100, 16-102 and 16-116 of the Election Law Declaring Valid the Designating Petitions purporting to Designate SAM SLOAN, NENAD BACH and GEETA RANKOTH as candidates for the Democratic Party nomination for Governor, Lieutenant Governor and Comptroller of New York State, respectfully at the Primary Election to be held at September 9, 2014 and restoring them to the Official Ballots of Such Primary Election

---

TO THE SUPREME COURT OF THE STATE OF NEW YORK:

COUNTY OF ALBANY

Your Petitioners by and through their attorney Neil Grimaldi by verified petition respectfully shows and alleges to this court.

1. That at all of the times hereinafter mentioned Sam Sloan, Candidate for the Democratic Party nomination for Governor, Nenad Bach Candidate for the Democratic Party nomination for Lieutenant Governor and Geeta Rankoth Candidate for the Democratic Party nomination for Comptroller of New York State are attempting to be candidates for the Democratic Party at the primary election to be held on September 9, 2014.

2. That at all times hereinafter mentioned the respondent New York State Board of Elections was and is charged with the responsibility of the supervision of the conduct of elections held in New York State including the duties of receiving and filing designating petitions for statewide public office and review and determination of objections and specifications of objections to such designating petitions, nullification of a determination of non-compliance, maintaining the permanent personal voter registration poll records of voters and the preparation of official Primary Election and General Election ballots for use in New York State Elections.

3. That on or about July 8, 2014 there were filed with the New York State Board of Elections certain papers allegedly constituting petitions purporting to designate for the September 9, 2014 Democratic Party Primary Election Sam Sloan, Candidate for the Democratic Party nomination for Governor, Nenad Bach Candidate for the Democratic Party nomination for Lieutenant Governor and Geeta Rankoth Candidate for the Democratic Party nomination for Comptroller of New York State. These petitions included more than 4000 numbered pages and were facially valid and regular with a cover sheet consistent with New York Election Law and the Rules of the Board of Elections of the State of New York..

4. Upon information and belief the said New York State Board of Elections improperly illegally and in

violation of the United States Constitution 14th Amendment due process clause and under the New York State Constitution at an official meeting on August 1, 2014 threw them off the ballot without ever informing Sam Sloan, Candidate for the Democratic Party nomination for Governor, Nenad Bach Candidate for the Democratic Party nomination for Lieutenant Governor and Geeta Rankoth Candidate for the Democratic Party nomination for Comptroller of New York State that there would be a hearing and determination of the validity of their petitions and the possibility of their signatures being invalidated.

5. The Comptroller Candidate Geeta Rankoth is 18 years of age and the law requires that the Comptroller be thirty years old. The Petitioners are seeking to have her replaced by the Committee on Vacancies, and not excluding these petitioners from having a candidate for Comptroller that represents the rights and duties of the designating petition which are to be respected and the practical viewpoints of the designating petition signers who have protected rights to have candidates of their choices.

6. New York State Election Law required that the candidates Sam Sloan, Nenad Bach and Geeta Rankoth have Objections filed against them for inadequate, improper or insufficient signatures before the Board invalidated the designating petitions under United States Law and the United States Constitution.

7. This was not done. Therefore there was no basis for the Board of Elections to invalidate their petitions, especially without giving them adequate notice as required by the United States Constitution 14th Amendment due process clause and New York Election Law and the required and regular procedures of the Board of Elections and the rules of the Board of Elections of the State of New York.

8. New York State election Law requires that a person who files Objections to the nominating petitions

of a candidate file within 6 days Specifications of their Objections; This was not done against the candidates Sam Sloan and Nenad Bach and Geeta Rankoth for inadequate signatures or improperly filed signatures other than the fact that the girl was 18 years old and therefore unqualified to be comptroller and the said attempts these candidates petitions and candidacy.

9. Since there were no proper Objections or Specifications of Objections and the fact that the cover sheet was in proper order as required by New York Election Law, the Board of Elections acted in a arbitrary and capricious manner in violation of the CPLR Article 78 and therefore their actions to invalidate the petitions of these candidates must be held null and void, especially in light of the fact that these three candidates, Sam Sloan, Nenad Bach and Geeta Rankoth never received notice as required by the due process clause of the Fourteenth Amendment that on Friday August 1, 2014 the New York State Board of Elections would consider the possibility of removing them from the ballot.

10. Had the Board of Elections properly informed Sam Sloan, Nenad Bach and Geeta Rankoth, they would have had an opportunity to defend their petitions, an opportunity which was illegally and unfairly denied them and as a violation of the due process clause of the 14th amendment because the hearings were unjust and because these candidates were required to be given notice under the United States Constitution 14th Amendment due process clause and New York Election Law and the rules and regulations and normal procedures followed by the New York Board of Elections.

11. The Democratic process requires that the voters have a choice of different candidates in the primaries. If Geeta Rankoth is excluded as a candidate there is no opponent for comptroller for Thomas P. DiNapoli.

12. The Board of Elections in the State of New York is intrinsically an unfair body in that they are

constituted in being selected by the two major parties , the Republican Party and the Democratic Party and this is so improper that the clients could not get a fair hearing. The fact that the Board of Elections is unfairly constituted warrants that the Board of Elections be deemed violative of the due process clause of the 14th Amendment and they should be disbanded and invalidated. Independent voters in the state of New York have no representation on the New York State Board of Elections. This is unfair because they constitute a larger group than the Republican Party.

13. It is intrinsically violative of the United States Constitution and the one-man-one-vote principle of federal election law makes it unconstitutional that the State Board of Elections does not include representatives of the other parties with ballot access, including the Green Party voters, Conservative Party voters, Independence Party voters and Working Families Party voters. Reynolds vs. Sims 377 US 533 established that the principle of the Equal Protection Clause and equal protection of the law required legislative voting to be based on population. The Board of Elections ignores this landmark case and principle. This case stands for the fundamental principle of representative government in the United States and is one for equal protection for equal number of people. The right to vote is a personal right and the idea that one group can be granted greater voting strength as the board does in excluding all not-Democratic and all non-Republican voters is hostile to the standards to popular representative government. Under the equal protection clause a claim of debasement of the right to vote through malapportionment presents a practicable controversy and the equal protection clause provides manageable standards for the lower courts to determine the constitutionality of state legislative approtionment.. Baker vs. Carr 369 US 186. See also Oliver vs. Board of Education, 306 F. Supp 1286, Atkins vs. Monahan, 91 Misc. 2d 499, 399 NYS 2d 166, Morris vs Board of Supervisors 50 Misc. 2d 929, 273 NYS 2d 453, Sergey v. King's County Republican Party 459 F.2d 308, See Morder v. Ogrlive 394 US 814, 89 S.Ct. 1493

WHEREFORE it is respectfully prayed that this court:

1. Declare sufficient and valid the designating petitions filed with the New York State Board of Elections purporting to designate and/or nominate Sam Sloan as Candidate for the Democratic Party nomination for Governor, Nenad Bach as Candidate for the Democratic Party nomination for Lieutenant Governor and Geeta Rankoth as Candidate for the Democratic Party nomination for Comptroller of New York State to be held on September 9, 2014 and

2. Order and decree and direct the New York State Board of Elections to restore the names of Sam Sloan, Nenad Bach and Geeta Rankoth to the ballot as Candidates for the Democratic Party nomination for Governor, Lieutenant Governor and Comptroller of New York State to be printed and placed on the official ballots to be used either at the September 9, 2014 Democratic Primary Election and the November 4, 2014 General Election and why the Petitioners should not have such other and further relief as to this curt may seem just and proper.

3. Petitioners seek to have the New York Board of Elections as presently organized and constituted declared null and void as violative of the United States Constitution and state and federal laws including the one-man-one-vote principle of the United States Constitution and federal law.

4. Award Petitioners Attorney's Fees

Respectfully Submitted,

Neil Grimaldi
Attorney for Candidates
2860 Buhre Avenue
Bronx NY 10461

646-229-7974

Sam Sloan

Candidate for New York Governor

17

STATE OF NEW YORK)
) ss:
COUNTY OF ALBANY)

VERIFICATION

I, the undersigned, the petitioner named in the foregoing petition, being duly sworn, says:

I have read the foregoing petition subscribed by me and know the contents thereof and the same is true of my own knowledge, except as to those matters herein stated to be alleged upon information and belief and as to those matters I believe it to be true.

Sam Sloan

Sam Sloan

On the 4th Day of August, 2014 before me personally came Samuel H. Sloan to me known to be the person described herein and who executed the foregoing instrument. Such person duly swore to such instrument before me and duly acknowledged that he executed the same.

Sheila Horton

NOTARY PUBLIC

SHEILA HORTON
Notary Public, State of New York
Qualified in Albany County
No. 01HO6153076
Commission Expires 9-20-2014

18

STATE OF NEW YORK)
) ss:
COUNTY OF ALBANY)

ATTORNEY'S VERIFICATION

Neil Grimaldi, an attorney duly admitted to the practice of law before the courts of New York does hereby affirm under penalties of perjury:

1. He is the attorney for the petitioners in this action.

2. He has reviewed the contents of this document with his clients and upon the conclusion of said review as to the facts herein believes the be the same to be true.

3. This affirmation is being used pursuant to the provisions of the CPLR and applicable case law due to the fact that time is of the essence and the petitioner and his counsel are in different counties. Counsel having officer in the county of Bronx and Petitioners residing in a county other than the county of the Bronx.

Neil Grimaldi
Attorney for Petitioners-Candidates
2860 Buhre Avenue
Bronx NY 10461
646-229-7974

On the 4th Day of August, 2014 before me personally came Neil V. Grimaldi to me known to be the person described herein and who executed the foregoing instrument. Such person duly swore to such instrument before me and duly acknowledged that he executed the same.

NOTARY PUBLIC

SHEILA HORTON
Notary Public, State of New York
Qualified in Albany County
No. 01HO6153076
Commission Expires 9-20-2014

19

STATE OF NEW YORK
OFFICE OF THE ATTORNEY GENERAL

ERIC T. SCHNEIDERMAN
ATTORNEY GENERAL

DIVISION OF STATE COUNSEL
LITIGATION BUREAU

Writer Direct: (518) 408-2009

August 6, 2014

Via Facsimile

The Honorable Andrew G. Ceresia
Justice of the Supreme Court
Supreme Court
County of Albany
16 Eagle Street
New York, New York 12207

Re: Sloan v. Kellner
Index No. 4003-2014
OAG No. 14-172547

Dear Justice Ceresia:

This Office hereby acknowledges receipt of the papers forwarded to us in the above-referenced matter pursuant to the notice requirements of Executive Law § 71 and C.P.L.R. 1012(b)(1) because there appears to be a purported constitutional challenge to a State statute.

Please be advised that, after careful consideration, this Office has determined that we will not be participating in the above-referenced matter at this time. Because there are many reasons why the Office of the Attorney General may decide not to participate, we respectfully suggest that no adverse inference regarding our view of the merits of the constitutional challenge to the State statute, or the nature of the State's interest, should be drawn from our non-participation at this stage.

This Office may choose to intervene at a later stage for purposes of defending the constitutionality of the statute. We note that, pursuant to Executive Law § 71 and C.P.L.R. 1012(b)(1), if this matter is appealed, the Office of the Attorney General must receive another notification of the constitutional challenge. We also would appreciate being advised of any final decision.

Thank you. I can be reached at (518) 408-2009 with any questions.

Respectfully submitted,

Helena Lynch

HELENA LYNCH
Assistant Attorney General

cc: Neil Grimaldi, Esq. (via United States First Class Mail)
Attorney for Petitioners
2860 Buhre Avenue
Bronx, New York 10461

STATE BOARD OF ELECTIONS
40 N. PEARL STREET
ALBANY, N.Y. 12207-2108
Phone: 518/474-2063 Fax: 518/486-6627
www.elections.ny.gov

August 7, 2014

AUG - 7 2014

Hon. Andrew G. Ceresia
Rensselaer County Courthouse
Troy, New York 12180

Via Facsimile Only: (518) 271-1047

Re: *Matter of Sloan, et al v New York State Board of Elections* (Index No: 4003-14)

Dear Judge Ceresia:

The State Board of Elections received a designating petition purporting to designate Sam Sloan a candidate of the Democratic Party for the office of Governor of the State of New York, Nenad Bach a candidate of the Democratic Party for the office of Lt. Governor of the State of New York, Neil V. Grimaldi a candidate of the Democratic Party for the office of New York State Attorney General and Geeta Rankoth a candidate of the Democratic Party for the office of New York State Comptroller.

Subsequently, General Objections and Specifications of Objections were filed by three different objectors with respect to the petition for Neil V. Grimaldi. One objector stated that the candidate claimed 5,113 signatures and that the actual number of valid signatures was zero. The second objector claimed that the petition contains 4,476 signatures, far short of the 15,000 needed. The third objector claimed that the petition does not contain the minimum number of signatures required and fails to contain signatures from one half of the congressional districts in the state as required.

In addition, General Objections and Specifications of Objections were filed by two objectors with respect to the petition for Geeta Rankoth. Both objectors claimed that the petition fails to contain the minimum number of signatures required, that the candidate does not meet the age requirement to hold the office, and that the candidate is not an enrolled member of the Democratic Party.

The Commissioners of the State Board met on August 1, 2014, at which time they made the determination that 4,087 signatures were filed and, therefore, the petition did not contain the 15,000 signatures required to secure the designations in question. The Board also determined that Geeta Rankoth did not meet the age requirement to hold the office of New York State Comptroller. By a unanimous vote of the Board the petitions for all four candidates were held invalid. (See attached Determinations.)

Subsequent to the Board's Determination, this proceeding to validate the designating petition was commenced in Albany Supreme Court. Notably, a separate proceeding to invalidate the designating petition of all four candidates was commenced in Albany Supreme Court on July 18, 2014 (*Cahill v Grimaldi, et al* [Index No. 3723-14]) and was returnable on August 4, 2014 before the Honorable Thomas J. McNamara. My understanding is that the *Cahill* matter was adjourned until today at 2:00 p.m.

Very truly yours,

Kathleen O'Keefe

Kathleen O'Keefe

Cc: Hon. Thomas J. McNamara
Via Facsimile Only: (518) 583-5335

Neil Grimaldi, Esq.
2860 Buhre Avenue
Bronx, NY 10461

AUG - 7 2014

FWC

FEATHERSTONHAUGH, WILEY & CLYNE, LLP
ATTORNEYS AND COUNSELLORS AT LAW

99 PINE STREET
ALBANY, NEW YORK 12207
WEBSITE: FWC-LAW.COM

FRANK G. HOARE
fgh@fwc-law.com

PHONE: (518) 436-0786
FAX: (518) 427-0452

August 7, 2014

Hon. Andrew G. Ceresia
Rensselaer County Courthouse
Troy, New York 12180

Via Facsimile Only: (518) 271-1047

Re: Matter of Sloan, et al v New York State Board of Elections (Index No: 4003-14)

Dear Judge Ceresia:

I am the attorney for New York State Comptroller Thomas DiNapoli. Comptroller DiNapoli was designated a candidate for the public office of Comptroller of the State of New York at a meeting of the Democratic State Committee on May 21, 2014. (See Certificate of Designation attached hereto).

I write in regard to the designating petition purporting to designate Sam Sloan a candidate of the Democratic Party for the office of Governor of the State of New York, Nenad Bach a candidate of the Democratic Party for the office of Lt. Governor of the State of New York, Neil V. Grimaldi a candidate of the Democratic Party for the office of New York State Attorney General and Geeta Rankoth a candidate of the Democratic Party for the office of New York State Comptroller.

General Objections and Specifications of Objections were timely filed by two objectors, Scott K. Bailey and Victor Antonio Perez with respect to the petition for Geeta Rankoth. Both objectors claimed that the petition fails to contain the minimum number of signatures required, that the candidate does not meet the age requirement to hold the office, and that the candidate is not an enrolled member of the Democratic Party. As such the assertion in the petition at paragraph 7, is false.

In response to the Objections, the Commissioners of the State Board of Election met on August 1, 2014, at which time they made the determination that 4,087 signatures were filed and, therefore, the petition did not contain the 15,000 signatures required to secure the designations in question. The Board also determined that Geeta Rankoth did not meet the age requirement to hold the office of New York State Comptroller. By a unanimous vote of the Board the petitions for all four candidates were held invalid. (See Determination dated August 1, 2014 attached hereto).

An objector is a necessary party to an action pursuant to Article 16 of the Election Law, and failure to name and serve an objector will result in dismissal. See Plochocki v. Onondaga County Board of Elections, 21 AD 3d 710 (4th Dept, 2005).

Here the Petitioners failed to name as a party and serve the Objectors. Accordingly, this action must be dismissed.

If you have any questions please do not hesitate to contact me.

Very truly yours,

Featherstonhaugh, Wiley & Clyne, LLP

Frank G. Hoare

FGH:

Attachments

State of New York
STATE BOARD OF ELECTIONS

August 1, 2014

STATE OF NEW YORK
STATE BOARD OF ELECTIONS

DETERMINATION

In the Matter of the objections of SCOTT K. BAILEY and VICTOR ANTONIO PEREZ to the Petition of the Democratic Party purporting to designate GEETA RANKOTH as a Candidate for the office of New York State Comptroller.

After an examination of the petition purporting to designate GEETA RANKOTH a candidate of the Democratic Party for the office of New York State Comptroller, and of the objections thereto, and the matter having been considered by the Commissioners of the State Board of Elections on August 1, 2014, it was determined that 4,087 signatures were filed, where 15,000 signatures are required to secure the designation in question. Further, specifications claim the designee does not meet the constitutional age requirement for the office being sought. Designee is 18 years of age, and the constitutional age requirement is 30. Therefore, the Board finds the petition is invalid.

Robert A. Brehm
Co-Executive Director

Todd D. Valentine
Co-Executive Director

FILED
NEW YORK STATE
BOARD OF ELECTIONS
ALBANY NEW YORK

2014 MAY 23 AM 9: 18

State of New York)
ss.:
County of Suffolk)

KRISTEN STAVISKY, being duly sworn, says that she is the Assistant Secretary of the State Committee of the Democratic Party of the State of New York, and acted as such at the meeting duly convened and held at the Hilton Long Island, 598 Broad Hollow Road, Melville, New York. on May 21-22, 2014, and that the statements in the foregoing Certificate are true.

Kristen Stavisky

State of New York)
ss.:
County of Suffolk)

On the 22nd day of May in the year 2014 before me, the undersigned, personally appeared, KRISTEN STAVISKY personally known to me or proved to me on the basis of satisfactory evidence to be the individual whose name is subscribed to the within instrument and acknowledged to me that she executed the same in her capacity, and that by her signature on the instrument, the individual, or the person upon behalf of which the individual acted, executed the instrument.

JEANINE RENEE JOHNSON
Notary Public, State of New York
No. 02JO6291597
Qualified in New York County
Commission Expires Oct. 15, 2017

Notary Public

FILED
NEW YORK STATE
BOARD OF ELECTIONS
ALBANY, NEW YORK

2014 MAY 23 AM 9:17

State of New York)
ss.:
County of New York)

DAVID A. PATERSON, being duly sworn, says that he is the State Chair of the State Committee of the Democratic Party of the State of New York, and acted as such at the meeting duly convened and held at the Hilton Long Island, 598 Broad Hollow Road, Melville, New York, on May 21-22, 2014, and that the statements in the foregoing Certificate are true.

David A. Paterson

State of New York)
ss.:
County of New York)

On the 22nd day of May in the year 2014 before me, the undersigned, personally appeared, DAVID A. PATERSON personally known to me or proved to me on the basis of satisfactory evidence to be the individual whose name is subscribed to the within instrument and acknowledged to me that he executed the same in his capacity, and that by his signature on the instrument, the individual, or the person upon behalf of which the individual acted, executed the instrument.

05-22-2014
BOUKIA FABRICE PARFAIT
Notary Public, State of New York
No. 01BO6297571
Qualified in New York County
Term Expires August 12, 2017

Notary Public

28

FILED
NEW YORK STATE
BOARD OF ELECTIONS
ALBANY, NEW YORK

2014 MAY 23 AM 9:17

CERTIFICATE OF DESIGNATION

The undersigned, David A. Paterson, State Chair and, Kristen Stavisky, Assistant Secretary of the State Committee of the Democratic Party of the State of New York ("State Committee") do hereby jointly and severally certify that, at a meeting of the State Committee duly convened and held at the Hilton Long Island, 598 Broad Hollow Road, Melville, New York, on May 21-22 2014, a quorum being present, a majority vote of the State Committee designated the following persons as candidates for the nominations of the Democratic Party of the State of New York for the statewide offices set forth opposite their names, such offices to be voted on at the Primary Election on September 9, 2014 and the November 4, 2014 General Election:

NAME OF CANDIDATE	RESIDENCE	OFFICE
Andrew M. Cuomo	4 Bittersweet Lane, Mt. Kisco, NY 10549	Governor
Kathy C. Hochul	405 Gull Landing Buffalo, New York 14202	Lieutenant Governor
Thomas P. DiNapoli	100 Great Neck Road, Great Neck Plaza, PO Great Neck, NY 11201	State Comptroller
Eric T. Schneiderman	645 West End Avenue Apt. 8F New York, NY 10025	Attorney General

We further certify that, at said meeting, the following persons were duly elected to serve as the committee to fill any vacancy in the foregoing designations:

Name:	Address:
Keith L.T. Wright	2225 Fifth Ave, Apt. ME New York, NY 10037
Sheila Comar	29 Depot Street, Middle Granville, NY 12849
Michael Reich	255 Breezy Way, Lawrence, NY 11559
Sherry Pavone	19 Fairwind Court, Northport, NY 11768

29

SUPREME COURT OF THE STATE OF NEW YORK
COUNTY OF ALBANY

In the Matter of the Application of Sam Sloan, as Candidate for Governor of the State of New York, Nenad Bach as Candidate for Lieutenant Governor of the State of New York, Geeta Rankoth as Candidate for Comptroller of the State of New York and Neil Grimaldi as Candidate for Attorney General of the State of New York

Petitioners-Candidates-Aggrieved

STATEMENT OF LAW

-against-

DOUGLAS A. KELLNER, ANDREW SPANO, JAMES A. WALSH and GREGORY P. PETERSON Commissioners and Constituting the NEW YORK STATE BOARD OF ELECTIONS

Respondents

Index No. 4003-14

ERIC T. SCHNEIDERMAN as Attorney General of the State of New York

---

For an Order Pursuant to Sections 16-100, 16-102 and 16-116 of the Election Law Declaring Valid the Designating Petitions purporting to Designate SAM SLOAN, NENAD BACH, GEETA RANKOTH and NEIL V. GRIMALDI as candidates for the Democratic Party nomination for Governor, Lieutenant Governor. Comptroller of New York State and attorney General of New York State respectfully at the Primary Election to be held at September 9, 2014 and restoring them to the Official Ballots of Such Primary Election

---

Neil Grimaldi, a New York attorney for the petitioner, states:

1) In **Board of Estimate of City of New York v. Morris** **489 U.S. 688 (1988)** decided: March 22, 1989, the United States Supreme Court held as I am seeking which is the law of the United States. The United States Supreme Court held the Board of Estimates was illegally constituted because it violated

the Equal Protection Clause of the 14th Amendment to the constitution. So, the New York Board of Estimates was found to be null and void as a government agency, citing Reynolds vs. Sims, 377 US 533 and Abate vs Muss, 403 US 182. The Board of Elections completely denies voter equality by ignoring the voting rights of all voters, not Republican or Democrat. Also, Republican Voters have more voting power than Democrats because Democrats far exceed Republican voters. The NY Board of Elections and the New York City Board of Elections violate the Equal Protection Clause based on the disparity between Republicans and Democrats and the fact that so many millions of voters have no representative on the Board of Elections. This inequitable system at the board places the most prejudicial people as executives or board members by how they are chosen by representatives of the Democratic Party Chairperson and Republican Party Chairperson. Therefore, they cannot constitute a just body or forum to make legal and binding decisions.

This year at a recent July 2014 hearing of the New York City Board of Elections, Eliot Quinones was placed on the ballot by the clerk's report. Then without notice a new Board of Elections clerk's report put him off the ballot. These decisions excluded voters who properly signed the petition. New York Board of Elections clerk's report fundamentally put him off the ballot based on improper decisions excluding voters who properly signed the petition. The New York City Board of Elections also allows one representative and one representative for Brooklyn despite the fact that Brooklyn has three times as many voters as Richmond. This is exactly the reason why the Board of Estimates was found illegal by the United States Supreme Court. The Board of Elections in the City of New York is part of the New York State Board of Elections.

2) Reynolds vs Sims, 377 US 533 established that the Fourteenth Amendment of the United States Constitution established the principle of the equal protection clause and equal protection of the law. Required the Alabama legislature voting to be based on population. The Board of Elections ignores this landmark case and principle. This case stands for the fundamental principle of legislative government in the United States of equal representation for equal numbers of people. The right to vote is a personal right. The idea that one group can be granted greater voting strength as the board does excluding all Democratic and Republican voters than another is inconsistent with standards for popular representative government. Under the equal protection clause a claim of debasement of the right to vote through mal apportionment represents a practicable controversy. And the equal protection clause provides manageable standards for the lower courts to determine the constitutionality of a state legislative appointment scheme, citing Baker vs. Carr, 361 US 186. In addition it undercuts states

voters rights and the duly established United States Constitutional rights.

3) Oliver vs. Board of Education, 306 F. Supp. 1286, No. 69 Civ 2130, United States District Court for the Southern District of New York held that a statute creating the New York City School Board was unconstitutional where the statute provided that citizens of each borough elected one member of the school board. Statute diluted votes of the most populous boroughs. The way the New York State Board of Elections and New York City Board of Elections is organized violates the rights of all voters not Republican or Democratic and gives each Republican voter more power than each Democrat which is unequal and illegal. Also, voting procedures including proxy voting must follow one man one vote Atkins v. Monahan, 91 Misc. 2d 499, 399 NYS 2d 166.

4) Sergey v. King's County Republican Party, 459 F.2d 308 invalidated a county political party's rule on the voting procedure of the one party where each county committee member has an equal vote weighed according to the number of Republican voters in the district he represents. This violates the one-man one-vote principle established by the Supreme Court as a voters constitutional right. The amount of Democratic Party voters far exceeds the amount of Republican Party voters and gives one Republican and Democratic members equal power and not representing all other voters and Republican or Democratic violated the one-man one-vote constitutional law principle. The equal protection clause applies one man one vote even to count committeemen. Not giving a group the right to representation violates their constitutional rights and discriminates against them. See Moder v. Ogilive 394 US 814, 89 S.Ct. 1493

5) Fisher vs. Board of Supervisors, 59 Misc. 953; 301 NYS 2d 310 citing Seaman v. Fedourich, 16 NY 2d 94, 101 required the "one man one vote" principle required each votes be given equal weight. The Board of Elections excludes the rights of millions of voters and unfairly gives Republican voters more importance than an equal number of Democratic voters. See Burton vs. Schmidt, 128 Misc. 270.

6) The basic exclusion of the Board of Elections of the rights of millions of voters not Republican and Democrat is unequitably a violation of the equal protection clause of the Fourteenth Amendment see Reynolds vs. Sims, supra, Board of Estimates vs. Morris, supra.

7) The New York City Board of Elections has a long history of violating the United States voter's rights and insurgent Democratic and Republican voters rights including none of the other parties by the illegal

manner that members of the Board of Elections in New York City as elsewhere are chosen by the New York City Republican and Democratic Party political readers. This violates the Fourteenth Amendment due process requirements because the forum is not a just body and it is constituted in a way by giving undue and improper power to representatives of the Democratic and Republican Chairmen and their representatives who claim to me made a quasi-judicial body making legally binding decisions which they have harmful by their extensive officer and bureau members are selected illegally by the Political Democratic Party Chairmen and Republican Chairmen. It would be proper and legal only to have a civil service Board of Elections. The members of the Board of Electioms or an independent non-partisan non-prejudicial system of choosing Board of Election members statewide and in New York City and in each of our great New York County.

8) <u>The Respondents have refused to provide a legal basis in opposition to this motion because there is none.</u>

Whereas Petitioner is requesting an opportunity to subpoena witnesses and present evidence about the long history of political corruption caused by the illegal and improper manner the New York State Board of Elections and New York City Board of Elections are illegally formed, violative of the equal protection clause one man one vote and basic justice

DATED: August 8, 2014
Bronx, New York

Neil Grimaldi, Esq.
Attorney for Petitioners-Candidates
2860 Buhre Avenue, 1E
Bronx NY 10461

646-229-7974

SUPREME COURT OF THE STATE OF NEW YORK
COUNTY OF ALBANY

In the Matter of the Application of SAM SLOAN, as Candidate for Governor of the State of New York, NENAD BACH as Candidate for Lieutenant Governor of the State of New York, GEETA RANKOTH as Candidate for Comptroller of the State of New York and NEIL V. GRIMALDI as Candidate for Attorney General of te State of New York

Petitioners-Candidates-Aggrieved

-against-

DOUGLAS A. KELLNER, ANDREW SPANO, JAMES A. WALSH and GREGORY P. PETERSON Commissioners and Constituting the NEW YORK STATE BOARD OF ELECTIONS
Respondents

ERIC T. SCHNEIDERMAN as Attorney General of the State of New York

AFFIDAVIT AND MOTION TO TO SET ASIDE EVIDENCE SUBMITTED BY RESPONDENTS

Index No. 4003-14

For an Order Pursuant to Sections 16-100, 16-102 and 16-116 of the Election Law Declaring Valid the Designating Petitions purporting to Designate SAM SLOAN, NENAD BACH, GEETA RANKOTH and NEIL V. GRIMALDI as candidates for the Democratic Party nomination for Governor, Lieutenant Governor, Comptroller and Attorney General of New York State, respectfully at the Primary Election to be held at September 9, 2014 and restoring them to the Official Ballots of Such Primary Election

---

TO THE SUPREME COURT OF THE STATE OF NEW YORK:

COUNTY OF ALBANY

Neil Grimaldi, a New York Attorney for the petitioners, states the following:

1. The Evidence submitted by the respondent New York Board of Elections must be set aside by this Court because the Designating Petitions submitted by respondents were not original as required by New York State Laws of Evidence. The originals were 8.5 x 14 on green paper but the board submitted 8.5 x 11 copies, photo reduced.

2. The original petitions are in possession of the respondent and there was no basis for the original petitions not to be submitted, especially when the size and shape of the petitions are a major question of fact in this case.

3. The original petitions were on green color paper 8.5 x 14 and on card stock and not on these 8.5 x 11 reduced xeroxed photocopies which you can see are not originals.

4. The Court can clearly see that the designating petitions submitted by respondent are not original but are reduced copies.

5. Since the evidence submitted by respondents of the designating petitions have to be set aside, because they are not the original documents submitted by the petitioners, which original designating petitions are in the possession of the respondents at their office at 40 N. Pearl Street, which are only a few blocks from this court, there is no basis or reason the originals were not submitted as

required by law. The respondents have failed to submit adequate or sufficient evidence to undermine or invalidate the United States constitutional protected rights of the signers of these petitions and the rights of these candidates to be on the ballot. Judgment must be rendered for petitioners in this case so that the petition signers have a Constitutional protected right to have the candidates of their choice on the the ballot, which are SAM SLOAN, as Candidate for Governor of the State of New York, NENAD BACH as Candidate for Lieutenant Governor of the State of New York, GEETA RANKOTH as Candidate for Comptroller of the State of New York and NEIL V. GRIMALDI as candidate for Attorney General of New York. See Reynolds vs. Sims 377 US 533, Baker vs. Carr, 369 US 186 and Board of Estimate of City of New York v. Morris 489 U.S. 688 (1988).

6. The fact that the original petitions were 8.5 x 14 and on green paper and on card stock are not what respondents submitted which were 8.5 by 11 reduced photocopies, the acts of the respondents would appear to be fraudulent on the evidence they submitted especially considering the size of the petitions is such a crucial element of this case.

7. Sam Sloan, the petitioner, a very credible individual, testified that he was a math major at the University of California at Berkeley, is a book publisher and reprinter of more than 550 titles, and was the last non-lawyer ever to argue a case orally before the United

States Supreme Court, in a case that he won. SEC vs. Samuel H. Sloan, 436 US 103 (1978).

8. The unrefuted testimony of Sam Sloan as to how the proceedings at the Board of Elections took place clearly indicate that there were no witnesses or testimony regarding these candidates at the meeting of the Board of Elections on August 1, 2014 which would warrant them being placed off the ballot.

9. The only evidence was submitted by an attorney, Kimberly Galvin, and not by a witness.

10. Miss Galvin was not sworn in as a witness.

11. Miss Galvin did not testify in an adequate matter as to justify the boards actions.

12. Also, notice was required to the party who may be damaged by the actions of the Board.

13. The board acted based on Miss Galvin's statements. The board was as required by law to review the documents which was also a violation of the 14th Amendment due process clause which they did not do according to Sam Sloan's unrefuted testimony.

14. There were no Objections or Specifications as required by the New York Election Law Section 16-102 to the candidates at the board of election meeting against or in regard to Sam Sloan, Nenad Bach and Neil Grimaldi.

15. At the trial the only specifications entered into evidence concerned Geeta Rankoth. The evidence submitted to the board of elections at their hearing did not justify or substantiate their actions to invalidate any candidate on this slate.

16.Therefore there was insufficient evidence. This also shows that the board is a prejudiced body doing in the work of the Republican and Democratic State Chairman which is also a violation of the due process clause of the 14th Amendment. This is further reason why the board should be held unconstitutional because it is not a fair body or forum and does not properly represent all the voters of the state of New York. See Reynolds vs. Sims, supra and Baker vs. Carr, supra and Board of Estimate of City of New York v. Morris supra.

17. Miss Kimberly Galvin, an employee of Respondent Board of Elections, should have been called as a witness to refute the testimony of Sam Sloan. His unrefuted testimony clearly proves that the board acted unconstitutionally at its meeting on August 1, 2014 when these candidates were improperly and illegally put off the ballot. There is an inference that the court can draw against the

Board of Elections for their failure to call Miss Kimberly Galvin who was a witness to what happened at the Board of Elections meeting and her office is only a few blocks away. There are inferences to be drawn against the Board of Elections by their failure to produce the original designating petitions. At the hearing on August 11 there was a executive of the board of elections who could have been called to refute the testimony of Sam Sloan but was not called. There is an inference to be drawn from the failure to call this witness that Sam Sloan's testimony was truthful, which testimony was sufficient to invalidate the proceedings of the Board of Elections at their meeting on August 1 which invalidated these candidates without hearing any evidence or testimony against this slate of candidates, because there was no evidence or testimony to justify their actions. The Board of Elections failed to produce a brief or any case law to counter petitioners request to invalidate the Board of Elections. See Reynolds vs. Sims, supra and Baker vs. Carr, supra and Board of Estimate of City of New York v. Morris supra.

18. I move herein to add my name Neil Grimaldi as a petitioner and as a candidate for attorney general based on the fact that it was only a clerical mistake not to put me on as a petitioner in this case. Adding my name as petitioner in this case is consistent with my signing the motion as an attorney for the petitioners.

19. MY name as a petitioner is on the Statement of Law Submitted

heretofore.

20. The respondent is not prejudiced by my name being submitted as a candidate for Attorney General.

21. The meeting of the board of Elections on August 1, 2014 had no evidence submitted to invalidate me as an Attorney General candidate so therefore there is no basis to exclude me as an Attorney General candidate.

22. The petitioner signer's constitutional rights to have me as an attorney general candidate would be violated as the result of a clerical omission and that would be unconstitutional. Reynolds vs. Sims, supra and Baker vs. Carr, supra and Board of Estimate of City of New York v. Morris supra.

DATED: August 11, 2014
Bronx, New York

Neil Grimaldi, Esq.
Attorney for Petitioners-Candidates
2860 Buhre Avenue, 1E
Bronx NY 10461

646-229-7974

STATE OF NEW YORK
SUPREME COURT COUNTY OF ALBANY

In the Matter of the Application of Sam Sloan, as Candidate for Governor of the State of New York, Nenad Bach as Candidate for Lieutenant Governor of the State of New York, Geeta Rankoth as Candidate for Comptroller of the State of New York and Neil Grimaldi as Candidate for Attorney General of the State of New York,

Petitioners-Candidates-Aggrieved,

-against- Index No. 4003-14

DOUGLAS A. KELLNER, ANDREW SPANO, JAMES A. WALSH and GREGORY P. PETERSON Commissioners and Constituting the NEW YORK STATE BOARD OF ELECTIONS,

Respondents

ERIC T. SCHNEIDERMAN as Attorney General of the State of New York

---

For an Order Pursuant to Sections 16-100, 16-102 and 16-116 of the Election Law Declaring Valid the Designating Petitions purporting to Designate SAM SLOAN, NENAD BACH, GEETA RANKOTH and NEIL V. GRIMALDI as candidates for the Democratic Party nomination for Governor, Lieutenant Governor, Comptroller of New York State and Attorney General of New York State respectfully at the Primary election to be held at September 9, 2014 and restoring them to the Official Ballots of Such Primary Election

---

- E L E C T I O N P R O C E E D I N G S -

BEFORE: HON. ANDREW G. CERESIA,
Acting Justice of the Supreme Court

Transcript of the Proceedings held on the record on August 11, 2014, at the Albany County Courthouse, Albany, New York.

APPEARANCES:

NEIL GRIMALDI, ESQ.
2860 Buhre Avenue, Suite 1E
Bronx, New York 10461
Attorney for Petitioners-Candidates-Aggrieved

STATE OF NEW YORK STATE BOARD OF ELECTIONS
40 North Pearl Street, Suite 5
Albany, NY 12207-2729
By: KATHLEEN O'KEEFE, ESQ.
Attorneys for Respondent
New York State Board of Elections

THE COURT: The Court calls the case of the matter of Sam Sloan, et al, versus the Commissioners of the New York State Board of Elections, et al.

If I could ask counsel to state their appearances for the record at this time.

MR. GRIMALDI: I wouldn't go before distinguished counsel.

MS. O'KEEFE: Kathleen O'Keefe, counsel to the State Board of Elections.

MR. GRIMALDI: Neil Grimaldi. I gave her my address. 2860 Buhre Avenue, the Bronx. Thank you.

THE COURT: Okay. Mr. Grimaldi, whom do you have seated with you at counsel's table?

MR. GRIMALDI: This is the petitioner, Mr. Sam Sloan.

Please stand up, sir.

He's also the candidate for Governor. He's also the Petitioner. He signed the Verified Petition.

THE COURT: Okay. Thank you. The Court has reviewed all of the papers submitted on behalf of the Petitioners, as well as the papers submitted in opposition thereto.

The Court scheduled this matter for a hearing, however, in order to give each side, if they wish, the opportunity to be heard further in connection with their papers and/or present any evidence.

Certainly each party can rest on their papers if they would like, but with that said, Mr. Grimaldi, at this time do you wish to be heard any further and/or present any evidence to the Court in connection with this matter?

MR. GRIMALDI: Since I made such a long trip, I would like to say something short.

THE COURT: Sure.

MR. GRIMALDI: I cannot see any basis in law that the Board of Elections is in existence. It totally violates the United States Constitution. I have cited the case of Morris versus -- the Morris case, where the Board of Estimate was invalidated in New York City. Also invalidated the Board of Elections. So the Board of Elections no longer exist in New York.

I have a very deep love and affection for our democratic process. This process, one person, one vote, is very, very serious matter. At the New York City Board of Elections, which is part of this system, you know, it's a very, very corrupt system. It's an incredibly corrupt system unfortunately. I'm not saying the People are corrupt, but the system is corrupt, as indicated by the amount of cases that have to get reversed by the Court.

Now, I mentioned a case in my papers where I went to the Board of Elections, the man was valid on the ballot. He was Elliot Quinones. I mentioned his name. He was valid on the ballot and then they played a game on me. They went through petition signatures again. Somebody wanted to knock him off. So they knocked him off. Then I filed a motion, Order To Show Cause, and there were serious complications, but I had to go -- the new law of the Court of Appeals required me to go through every one of the petitions, signatures I was trying to get back.

And what they did was they invalidated him based on forgery. They had no right to do that. That has to be sent to the Court. They threw out signatures for an alteration. The alteration was just an alteration of the county. There wasn't, you know, an alteration has to be by a signature of the subscribing witness. There is a whole long process of cases that I represented. I represented insurgents in the Bronx and in Queens. And I constantly see that the Board is acting in an inappropriate manner. And that's totally an unfair system where the chairman of the political parties select the members of the Board. It's totally unconscionable. The most prejudice of people are on the Board.

Furthermore, in the Board of Estimate case, it's the same situation we have here with the New York City Board of Elections and the State Board of Elections. One man, one vote.

In the state there are so many more Democrats than Republicans. So the Republican has the same representation as the Democrat. That's totally unconscionable and in violation of the equal protection clause and one man one vote in the 14th Amendment.

In New York City the same thing exists, one man, one vote. One vote in Staten Island has the same equivalent of three to four Democrats in Brooklyn. The whole consciousness of this whole system is totally invalid. And then they bring forth -- these people then invite and bring in inspectors. Inspected by political clubs.

I ran for office of the District Attorney of the Bronx. I ran for various offices. I couldn't possibly confront the fraud that exists there. I once sectioned where I won the thing, but it was overturned. I couldn't afford. I'm a poor man, your Honor. I couldn't afford an inspector in every section. That would cost me in fifteen hundred people. I couldn't afford fifteen hundred people.

The law is very clear here, your Honor. And I have the greatest respect for counsel here and the other female counsel for the Board of Elections, but they didn't even respond, your Honor. There is no response to these papers. There is no case against that.

Furthermore, in this particular matter, as the papers clearly indicate, Mr. Sam Sloan, who is a publisher and very honorable gentleman, submitted signatures. There was no objections filed as required by Election Law and there was no specifications filed against his signatures.

He's entitled to due process of law of a notice. They didn't follow the law in throwing him off. They can't just throw you off unless they go through the proper procedures. This is a constitutionally invalid way of throwing him off.

On the second candidate. He has a candidate he put up unfortunately was too young, but there was no objections to her signatures.

I'm asking that your Honor throw her off, but the point that we get a chance to, through the vacancy committee, find another candidate.

I was a candidate for Attorney General. There was specifications filed against -- objections filed against me and specifications filed against me. I'm not saying there weren't in this particular situation.

So that situation -- the situation is different regarding the various candidates, your Honor. I'm not saying that they acted properly against me. All I'm saying is that which was filed against me in that form was a proper form. We had, as you know, your Honor, we had Mr. Cahill, who was a Republican, brought a case against to throw me off, but he withdrew the thing, as you know. So this is the only case pending.

We are asking that the voters get a chance to have a choice of candidates. That if I get thrown off as Attorney General, there is no choice for the Democratic Party. If Mr. Sloan gets thrown off, he gets denied his rights.

If the Comptroller candidate, this young lady gets thrown off, the Comptroller candidate for the Democratic Party has no choice for candidates.

The Federal Election Law -- I have had many Federal Election Law cases. The voters have the right to have their people heard and their candidates of their choice put up.

Mr. Sam Sloan is a very unique candidate. He has a very distinctive philosophy from many of the other candidates and I'm asking that he be given his opportunity, because the way they threw him off wasn't fair.

Your Honor, I also want to thank you very much for your graciousness, your Honor. I am very proud to be before you and I have had contacts with your staff and you have been most graciously kind in regard to this matter and I want to thank you most humbly for coming here and being here with us.

I'm not going to say it, but I'm very proud that I'm an Italian American, like you, your Honor. But I have to also say that I am so proud as America we have three of the most Irish judges here, like Judge Connolly. And I'm so proud to come to this Court and see such honorable, outstanding men who represent our government and justice fairly. And I thank you very much, your Honor, for the opportunity to be heard.

THE COURT: Okay. Thank you, Mr. Grimaldi.

Miss O'Keefe, do you wish at this time to be heard and/or present any evidence to the Court?

MS. O'KEEFE: Thank you, your Honor.

I do have a certified record of the petition in this case, a copy of the petition itself, as well as the general and specific objections that were filed.

There are a couple of things that I want to just bring, factual things I want to bring to the Court's attention.

THE COURT: Before you do that, would you like to offer those items into evidence?

MS. O'KEEFE: I would. I have it here. I have it separated out and I have a copy for Mr. Grimaldi.

THE COURT: If you could provide a copy to Mr. Grimaldi, and then we will have the other set marked for identification, please.

MS. O'KEEFE: As I said, this is the petition itself. You might want to have three exhibits. I don't know how you want to do this.

One is the general objection form for -- and it's specific for a Scott Bailey. And those are the objections against the petition for Geeta Rankoth. And that was the New York State Comptroller candidate.

And then we have the general and specific objections for Victor Perez. And these are objections also against Geeta Rankoth. So there was two objectors with respect to that candidate.

And then here is my certification on top.

THE COURT: Okay. And the petitions themselves are included there?

MS. O'KEEFE: This is the big stack, the petition right here.

THE COURT: Okay. We will have the petitions -- we will have each of the documents marked separately as you have identified them.

MS. O'KEEFE: So the record is clear, the petition has four volumes.

MR. GRIMALDI: Judge, I'm going to object.

THE COURT: Let me have them marked for identification and then I will give you a chance to be heard, okay?

MR. GRIMALDI: Of course, your Honor.

(Respondent's Exhibits 1 through 4 marked for identification.)

THE COURT: Mr. Grimaldi, the respondents have sought to introduce Exhibits 1 through 4. They have been identified for the record. Do you have any objection to the Court receiving those exhibits at this time?

MR. GRIMALDI: Yes, your Honor. Do you want me to stand?

THE COURT: You are fine.

MR. GRIMALDI: I have a little problem with my legs, your Honor.

THE COURT: You can remain seated.

What's your objection?

MR. GRIMALDI: One, my objections were the ones I set out in my motion, right, and my paperwork for constitutional basis.

One, that the Board of Elections improperly organized it. I don't think they have authority to do anything in regard to these. I think they are an invalid institution and they have no authority to do what, in fact, they did. One.

Two. There is no -- your Honor, I don't want to go any further without complimenting counsel. It's such a privilege how she presented this and the manner she did, but there is no objection against me here, your Honor. In the papers there is no specifications against me as required by the law of the State of New York.

There is objections here filed against Miss Geeta Rankoth, but there is no specifications against her. The law requires objections and specifications.

The other papers are that was objections by Victor Perez.

There is an objector Scott Bailey against the same individual, Geeta Rankoth, but there is no -- I have no specifications filed here.

So, therefore, I think that they are defective. And I also think, since there is no specifications or objections against my other candidate, including Mr. Sloan, the other candidate, Nenad Bach, I think that you have to leave them on.

THE COURT: Okay. I understand your objections. Those objections are overruled.

At this time the Respondent's 1 through and including 4 will be marked into the record at this time.

(Respondent's Exhibits 1 through 4 received in evidence.)

THE COURT: Ms. O'Keefe, you may continue at this time.

MS. O'KEEFE: Yes. I did move, in case the Court has only allowed them to be marked, I move them into evidence as a business record of the Board.

THE COURT: Okay. They have been received at this time.

MS. O'KEEFE: Thank you.

With respect to the facts Mr. Grimaldi has raised, I would like to clarify a few things for the Court.

As we have already mentioned with the Exhibit 2 and 3, there are general and specific objections against the candidate Geeta Rankoth. And it was in the letter that I sent to the Court, as well as to Mr. Grimaldi.

Those objections had basically alleged, and they are in the record, that she did not have the minimum number of signatures required, that she did not meet the age requirement for the office, and that she was not an enrolled member of the Democratic Party.

With respect to that particular candidate, the Board received time specific and general objections from two different objectors. And when the Board met on August 1st, the Board voted in public, and they are on a video that's available on YouTube, because they do have their meetings in public, with respect to that candidate, that she did not meet both the signature requirements, as well as the age requirement, and they held her Petition invalid. So that's a separate issue with regard to that candidate.

With respect to Mr. Grimaldi, Mr. Grimaldi's papers, his Order To Show Cause and his Petition to validate the Petition, does not ask for relief with respect to Mr. Grimaldi at all.

The application is only with respect to the three

other candidates. So there is no request before the Court whatsoever for affirmative relief with respect to Mr. Grimaldi's candidacy for Attorney General. So that's the other factual piece I wanted to bring to the Court's attention.

With respect to the other two candidates, that would be Mr. Sloan and that would be Nenad Bach. There were no general and specific objections filed with respect to those two candidates, however, in Election Law 6-154, the very first paragraph, and this is the section that deals with objections, and the objections are addressed in subdivision two.

But in subdivision one, and it's only one sentence, so I would like to read it to the Court.

Any petition filed with the officer or board charged with the duty of receiving it, shall be presumptively valid.

And this is the operative language.

If it is in the proper form and appears to bear the requisite number of signatures authenticated in the manner prescribed by the chapter.

So that's in the first subdivision of that section, because as an initial matter, the Board of Elections looks at the Petition to see is it in the proper form and appears to bear the requisite number of signatures. So the Board can do that on their own. It's a facial review of the Petition.

Subdivision two goes to objections that are thereafter filed.

Once the Petition has passed that first test, that facial test, it's presumptively valid, it passes the facial test, gets put in the valid category, and then unless objections come in, it's a valid petition.

In this instance, and the Court has the Petition before it, the Petition needed to contain 15,000 signatures.

Now, there are a number of infirmities in the Petition, but the most important issue here is that the Petition itself does not even contain 5,000 signatures. You don't have to look at individual signatures here. That is the total world of signatures.

So the Board didn't have to go through their records. They didn't have to identify a voter and then look and see how they registered, anything like that.

In order to be on the statewide ballot in a Designated Petition, you must have 15,000 signatures.

I had sent the Court my letter explaining the process that I just put on the record and pointing out that in all three determinations, two based on the objectors that filed objections, and the third based on that prima facie review that the Board is entitled to do pursuant to that section and subdivision, the Board of Elections determined that there were only 4,087 signatures in this Petition, far short of the 15,000.

So that's the facts of what the Board did.

There are a couple other quick pieces of information I need to bring to the Court's attention.

The State Board's configuration is found in the Constitution. That is Article two, Section eight of the New York State Constitution, which requires that the Board is made up of representatives from the two major parties.

As we know, there are other states where only one party controls the Board of Elections. In New York it's a bipartisan system. It's meant to be a check on each side. So I just wanted to bring that section to the Court's attention.

And then last. The Board, as I mentioned, does hold their meetings in public. If there is any question that the Board was doing a prima facie review, as I mentioned in 6-154, subdivision two, then the video actually shows the motion that was made at the time and that the Board was actually identifying that section was the basis of what their determination was made.

I do have something here. I will tell the Court if you are at all interested where to find that video. But I wanted to make that clear. I sent the Court the determination. Mr. Grimaldi has the same, but the video is available on YouTube and you can see the actual motion that's being made in the video.

THE COURT: Okay. Thank you, ma'am.

MR. GRIMALDI: May I retort briefly?

THE COURT: Go right ahead.

MR. GRIMALDI: First of all, your Honor, if they acted improperly in regard to those issues that I mentioned, then the fact is that my signature, my candidacy for Attorney General, should also be validated if that was done in a proper manner.

Two. The fact that it's in the Constitution of the State of New York doesn't mean that they can violate the United States Constitution, which is clearly separate.

I filed the notice here on the Attorney General to show that I'm filing objections to the way this is organized. And that provision in the Constitution is an illegal provision in the Constitution and it should be invalid.

I gave you the cases, the Morris case, which is totally definitive on this issue. The government cannot put up one case, not one piece of paper, not one case to retort definitively what I set forth.

Honestly, your Honor, I think you have no other choice but to hold the Board of Elections as an unconstitutional body as pursuant to the United States Constitution and the cases that I specified, equal protection, due process, and one man one vote.

Thank you very much, your Honor.

THE COURT: Thank you, sir.

MR. GRIMALDI: Mr. Sloan would like to speak. He's the petitioner. He has a right to speak if you don't mind, your Honor.

MR. SLOAN: These petitions were marked as valid. There is a website, Board of Elections website, and these petitions, all the candidates, Nenad Bach, Sam Sloan and Neil Grimaldi and Geeta Rankoth, those petitions were marked valid. They remained valid until August 4th, which was just a few days ago.

Suddenly on August 4th the website changed from valid to invalid. From the date these petitions were filed, up until August 4th, which was just one week ago, they were listed as valid. If they were going to mark them invalid, they should have notified us of these documents, this stack of papers they gave us right now. This is the first time we have seen these documents. We have never seen these documents before.

By the way, I never saw the Petition. The Petitions were collected by community organizers. They were the people who went around and say would you like to have this candidate. They go around and ask these different people. They go around collecting signatures, put them all together, they filed them with the Board of Elections.

So actually I have never seen in my life. I have never seen the Petitions in these. I saw them in a bundle. Physically I saw them, but I never had a chance to go through.

Suddenly they are bringing all these big stack of papers into the board room and they are saying the Court is supposed to rule on this, where we have not actually seen these documents before. Never saw them.

And then Mr. Grimaldi filed his Order to Show Cause a week ago. They have not responded to that. I haven't seen any response at all, any written responses. If there is, I haven't received it.

MR. GRIMALDI: Your Honor, may I call him as a

witness for a minute, two minutes? He was a witness. It'll be two minutes.

THE COURT: Sure. That's fine.

MR. GRIMALDI: Get up on the witness stand.

THE COURT: If you are going to give sworn testimony, you have to get sworn in first.

THEREUPON,

SAM SLOAN,

called as a witness, having been first duly sworn, was examined and testified as follows:

DIRECT EXAMINATION

BY MR. GRIMALDI:

Q Mr. Sloan, can you tell us your background in terms of education and profession?

A Oh yeah. I was a math major at the University of California Berkeley. I'm a publisher. I published over 550 books. Mostly I reprint old, out-of-print books. And I was a securities trader. I actually won a case against the Securities Exchange Commission in the United States Supreme Court, SEC against Samuel H. Sloan, 436 US 103 1978.

About six months ago there was a big article, nationwide article, about me on all the major newspapers because my case, which I argued orally pro se, was the last time any nonlawyer has ever been allowed to argue before the

United States Supreme Court. They made a rule pro se people cannot argue anymore. So that's why my picture was in the newspaper about six months ago. You can look it up. But the case is 1978. That's a long time ago.

But again, so I'm a book publisher. I have argued and won a case in the United States Supreme Court.

Q Can you tell us some classic books that you published?

MS. O'KEEFE: Your Honor, objection. This is completely irrelevant to the Election Law matter.

THE COURT: Sustained.

BY MR. GRIMALDI:

Q You were at the Board of Elections, their proceedings? Discuss what happened.

A I was at the meeting. It was not a hearing. It was a meeting on August 1st. And at that meeting a list of decisions had been made. It was a motion to make certain decisions about the Board. They read off the list of candidates and they were saying that these candidates we have determined they don't have enough signatures or for some reason there is an objection and we are removing those candidates.

And the Board voted on that and voted to remove those candidates. Then after that happened, Miss

Kimberly, a lawyer by the name of Kimberly, said we have some additional people we want to remove from the ballot. And then they read the names of the four candidates, myself and Nenad Bach and Geeta Rankoth and Neil Grimaldi.

And they said we want to add these people to the list of people we are throwing off the ballot and the Board said so moved and it passed.

I don't think the Board had ever seen these Petitions or these candidates listed. I personally have never seen the Petition. I did see them physically as a stack of papers, but as far as being able to look through them or leaf through them, this is the first time in my life I have ever seen them. They didn't serve these documents on us. We never had a chance to review them. I don't know where they got that count from, four thousand, five thousand votes, signatures. I don't know how many signatures are in there, because I didn't collect the signatures. Volunteers collected the signatures. Volunteers in the Bronx.

Q What kind of volunteers were they?

A Well, I will be perfectly frank with you. Many of the homeless shelters in the area, they give these ladies jobs, you know, give them some kind of work because they are homeless and they go around collecting signatures.

Q Now, let me ask you. Was there any evidence

presented at that hearing about regarding those petitions that you filed?

A No, none at all. There was not a single word was mentioned about the quality of the petitions, the number of petitions or anything. They just said -- Kimberly said, here is four more names we want to have people we want thrown off the ballot.

It was almost unbelievable, because the Board had just passed a motion with regard to specifications of objections. All these other people are thrown. They had objections filed against them.

These candidates did not have objections filed against them. So they are being thrown off without any general objections or specification objections and, of course, the specifications must be filed and general objections must be filed in three days. Specification must be filed in six days. No objections were filed in a timely basis against these candidates.

The one objection was against Geeta Rankoth. They mistakenly felt that she wasn't registered to vote. Actually, she had just become of legal age and she had just registered to vote. So they were mistaken about that too.

Q Looking at these petitions, prima facie, right, looking at those petitions, how many pages are there approximately?

A Roughly 4,000 pages there.

Q So prima facie, there could have been a sufficient amount of signatures to make up 15,000, right?

A Right. If all those signatures were good, there would be 15,000 signatures there.

Q There was no evidence filed at the hearing about the inadequacy at the hearing?

A There was no evidence, no even discussion. There was no discussion about the evidence, how many signatures there were. They didn't bring out the papers.

I have been to hearings before the Board of Elections and New York Board of Elections in the City of New York. And when somebody comes up --

MS. O'KEEFE: Your Honor, objection. The City of New York is not here before the Court.

THE COURT: Sustained.

A Okay. But, but, but anyway, these papers were not brought out. They were not shown to the Commissioners. The Commissioners didn't know that there was a big stack of papers or a small stack or two sheets of paper. They didn't know what they had.

So I don't think the Board actually knew what they were voting on.

And again, you can play this. I haven't seen it yet, but I'm sure it's on YouTube. It's going to come on YouTube. You can play the video over. And you can see what happens. You can see them voting to throw a bunch of candidates off the ballot. My candidates not included in the motion. And then suddenly at the end of the thing, they come back, oh yeah, we have four more candidates we want thrown off the ballot.

BY MR. GRIMALDI:

Q There was no evidence presented in that situation?

A No evidence of any kind.

Q And no petition?

A And no, they never saw the petition.

Q So the Board didn't see anything?

A Right.

Q Who testified? Miss Kimberly is a lawyer?

A Kimberly is a lawyer. She's the only one who spoke on this issue. No one else said anything.

MR. GRIMALDI: Thank you very much, your Honor.

THE COURT: Thank you.

Miss O'Keefe, any questions?

MS. O'KEEFE: Yes. Thank you, your Honor.

CROSS EXAMINATION

BY MS. O'KEEFE:

Q Mr. Sloan, you have just testified that you have not seen that Petition previously; is that correct?

A I saw them physically as a stack of paper, but I did not collect the signatures. I did not assemble them. Other people in my neighborhood did.

Q And you have also just testified on the record under, you have been sworn, you have testified that you do not know how many signatures are in this Petition?

A That's right. I don't know.

Q And with respect to --

THE COURT: Excuse me one second.

MR. GRIMALDI: I'm sorry about the phone.

THE COURT: Let's get that shut off.

BY MS. O'KEEFE:

Q So with respect to the stack of papers that are there, the four volumes, you just testified there are 4,000 pages in that petition?

A I don't know. I don't know how many. I haven't counted the pages. I haven't had a chance. I just note it was listed as having 4,000 pages.

Q So you don't know if it's actually 4,000?

A No, I don't know.

Q Mr. Sloan, are you aware of how many sheets of

paper are in a ream of paper? Are you aware of how many are in a ream? You buy paper, copy paper in reams?

A I suppose there is 500. I don't know.

Q That's right. And four thousand pages would be how many reams?

A I guess simple multiplication. It would be eight.

Q It would be eight. Does that stack of pages look like it's eight reams of paper?

A I'm not an expert on paper size.

MS. O'KEEFE: Your Honor, may I approach the witness?

THE COURT: You may.

MS. O'KEEFE: I would like to have Mr. Sloan look at the first volume of this petition.

THE WITNESS: Wait.

THE COURT: Hold on, sir. Let her -- let Miss O'Keefe ask a question. If your attorney has an objection, he may be heard on that.

BY MS. O'KEEFE:

Q Mr. Sloan, can you -- this is the first volume of the petition. Can you turn to page 14?

A Okay. This is page 14.

Q Page 14. Can you turn to the next page after page 14?

(Sam Sloan - Cross by Ms. O'Keefe)

A Eighteen.

Q So the page that followed page 14 is page 18?

A That's what it looks like.

Q Okay. Can you turn to the next page that follows 18?

A Okay.

Q What number is that?

A It says 22.

Q And can you turn to the next page after 22?

A Twenty-five.

Q Okay. So I don't want to take the Court's time and burden the Court with going through the entire Petition, but you have just testified that there are pages that are not sequential in this Petition; is that correct?

A Wait. Wait. The word sequential. I'm a mathematician by the way. I have a degree in mathematics from the University of California Berkeley.

Are you familiar with the Fibonacci series?

Q Mr. Sloan, I'm asking the questions, not you.

Is it true that the numbers in that Petition, that volume one, are not sequential?

You just testified it was 14, 18, 22, 25.

A Well, define sequential, because I have a different definition as a mathematician.

Q Are there gaps in the Petition pagination?

A According to what you just said there was one 14 and one was 18.

Q So would you agree there are gaps in the Petition's pagination?

A You are asking me to define the term of gaps and sequence. I just -- I just don't know. And I'm not sure what you are referring to actually.

MS. O'KEEFE: Thank you, Mr. Sloan. I will not burden the Court any further with this. It is in evidence. The Court can look at the Petition for itself.

BY MS. O'KEEFE:

Q With respect to the events that occurred at the meeting, would you agree or do you recollect that the Board of Elections commission has actually voted in several categories with respect to petitions?

MR. GRIMALDI: I object, your Honor. That's unclear. That's very broad, not clear.

MS. O'KEEFE: I will make that clearer.

THE COURT: Okay.

BY MS. O'KEEFE:

Q Mr. Sloan, did the Board vote in one category with respect to a facial review of the petitions?

A No, I'm sorry, I don't know the answer to that question.

Q Do you recall if the Board voted in a category with respect to specific objections that were filed against petitions?

A I'm sorry, I don't have a detailed recollection of these things. I mean, it's on the video someplace and we can play it, you know.

MS. O'KEEFE: I would like to get that exhibit from you and show you something else in the Petition.

Q This is volume four of the Petition.

A I would like to know why --

MR. GRIMALDI: Excuse me. Just answer the question, please.

BY MS. O'KEEFE:

Q Mr. Sloan, can you turn to the very last page of volume four? Can you tell the Court what the page number is at the bottom?

A 1402 it says.

Q And that is the last page of volume four; is that correct?

A Yes. It has no signature on it. So obviously there is something wrong there.

Q So you have testified that you believed there was

4,000 pages in this Petition, but that is the last page of the Petition, isn't it?

A It seems to be.

Q And that was, again, 1402?

A It says 1402.

MS. O'KEEFE: Thank you. I will take that exhibit back, Mr. Sloan.

BY MS. O'KEEFE:

Q Now, Mr. Sloan, you have said that you received no objections to your Petition; is that correct?

A That is correct.

Q Are you aware of any of the other candidates receiving copies of specific objections to their Petition?

MR. GRIMALDI: Objection. That's hearsay.

THE COURT: Overruled.

A Am I aware?

Q Are you aware of any specific objections being filed against any of the other three candidates?

A You just changed your question and asked a different question.

Q No. I said are you aware of any specific objections being filed against the other three candidates?

A No.

Q You are not aware of that. Okay.

MS. O'KEEFE: Thank you, your Honor. I have no further questions.

MR. GRIMALDI: I'm finished, your Honor. Thank you very much.

THE COURT: Sir, you may step down. Thank you.

Mr. Grimaldi, for the purpose of this hearing, do you rest at this time?

MR. GRIMALDI: Yes.

THE COURT: Miss O'Keefe, for the purpose of this hearing, do you rest at this time?

MS. O'KEEFE: Yes, I do, your Honor, with one caveat. I just want to direct the Court's attention to 6-154, subdivision one in the Election Law, which authorizes the prima facie review.

THE COURT: All right. I want to thank all counsel for your time today. The Court will, again, has already reviewed the papers evidence submitted. The Court will take into account everything that was set forth today on the record, along with the evidence that has been submitted here in this hearing. The Court will reserve at this time and issue a written decision and order. Thank you all for your time.

MS. O'KEEFE: Thank you, your Honor.

MR. GRIMALDI: Thank you very much, your Honor.

It's a real privilege to be here before you, your Honor. Send my regards to your clerk. Thank you very much.

THE COURT: Thank you, Mr. Grimaldi.

Thank you, Miss O'Keefe.

(Whereupon the proceedings were concluded.)

* * *

INDEX

PETITIONER'S WITNESSES

NAME	DIRECT	CROSS	REDIRECT	RECROSS
Sam Sloan	21	26	--	--

RESPONDENT'S EXHIBITS

NO.	DESCRIPTION	IDENT.	EVID.
1	Certification from Board of Elections	11	13
2	Objections of Victor Perez (general & specific) re Petition of Geeta Rankoth	11	13
3	Objections of Scott Bailey (general & specific) re petition of Geeta Rankoth	11	13
4	Four volumes of the Petition at issue	11	13

C E R T I F I C A T I O N

I, Tracie Pamela Hilton, C.S.R, R.P.R., a Senior Court Reporter for the Unified Court System, Third Judicial District of the State of New York, do hereby certify that I attended and reported the foregoing proceedings; that it is a true and accurate transcript of the proceedings had therein to the best of my knowledge and ability.

Tracie Pamela Hilton

Tracie Pamela Hilton
Certified Shorthand Reporter
Registered Professional Reporter

Dated: August 14, 2014

Made in the USA
Monee, IL
08 November 2026

67994724R00057